studysync®

Reading & Writing Companion

American Literature

UNIT 1

studysync

studysync.com

Send all inquiries to:
BookheadEd Learning, LLC
610 Daniel Young Drive
Sonoma, CA 95476

ISBN 978-1-97-016212-7

5 6 QSX 24 23

C

Student Guide

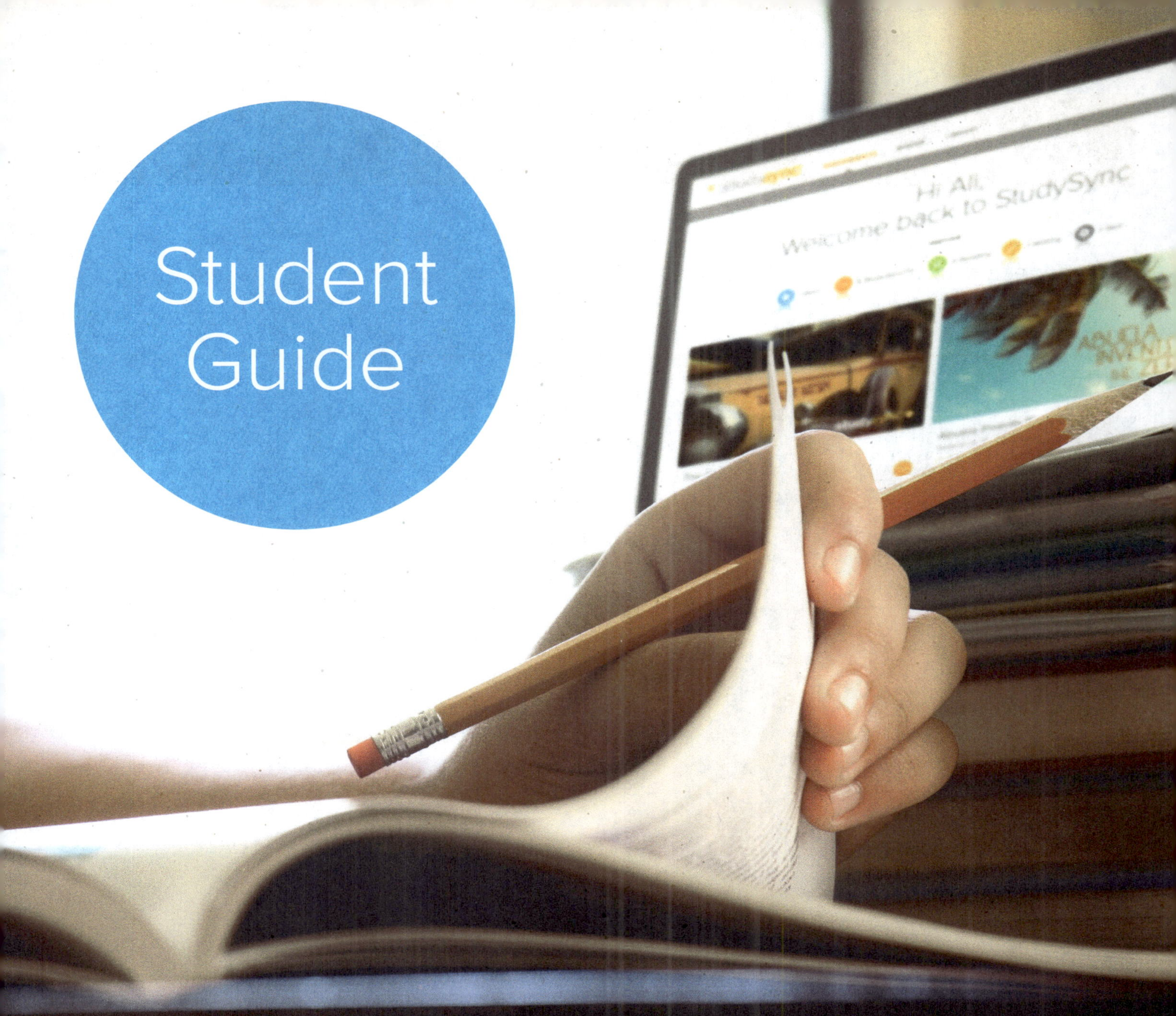

Getting Started

Welcome to the StudySync Reading & Writing Companion! In this book, you will find a collection of readings based on the literary focus of the unit you are studying. As you work through the readings, you will be asked to answer questions and perform a variety of tasks designed to help you closely analyze and understand each text selection. Read on for an explanation of each section of this book.

Close Reading and Writing Routine

In each unit, you will read texts and text excerpts that are from or are in some way connected to a particular period of American literature. Each reading encourages a closer look through questions and a short writing assignment.

Constitution of the Iroquois Nations

INFORMATIONAL TEXT
Dekanawidah (Oral Tradition)
Circa 1150

Introduction

Most information about Dekanawidah, co-founder of the Iroquois Confederacy, is lost to time. In Iroquois tradition, his name, meaning "two rivers flowing together," is used only under special circumstances. According to tradition, when the Iroquois tribes in present-day New York were torn apart by fighting, Dekanawidah stepped in to instill peace and unite the Iroquois nations. The oral constitution that followed represented an alliance among five tribes: the Seneca, Cayuga, Oneida, Onondaga, and Mohawk. A sixth tribe—the Tuscarora—later joined the union. Most historians believe that the democratic ideals of the Iroquois Constitution inspired the Constitution of the United States. The excerpt here includes about a dozen of the 117 total articles.

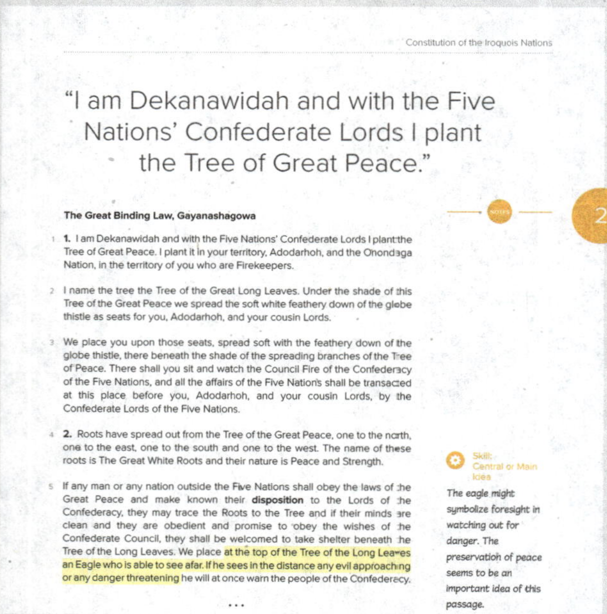

Constitution of the Iroquois Nations

"I am Dekanawidah and with the Five Nations' Confederate Lords I plant the Tree of Great Peace."

NOTES

The Great Binding Law, Gayanashagowa

1 **1.** I am Dekanawidah and with the Five Nations' Confederate Lords I plant the Tree of Great Peace. I plant it in your territory, Adodarhoh, and the Onondaga Nation, in the territory of you who are Firekeepers.

2 I name the tree the Tree of the Great Long Leaves. Under the shade of this Tree of the Great Peace we spread the soft white feathery down of the globe thistle as seats for you, Adodarhoh, and your cousin Lords.

3 We place you upon those seats, spread soft with the feathery down of the globe thistle, there beneath the shade of the spreading branches of the Tree of Peace. There shall you sit and watch the Council Fire of the Confederacy of the Five Nations, and all the affairs of the Five Nations shall be transacted at this place before you, Adodarhoh, and your cousin Lords, by the Confederate Lords of the Five Nations.

4 **2.** Roots have spread out from the Tree of the Great Peace, one to the north, one to the east, one to the south and one to the west. The name of these roots is The Great White Roots and their nature is Peace and Strength.

5 If any man or any nation outside the Five Nations shall obey the laws of the Great Peace and make known their **disposition** to the Lords of the Confederacy, they may trace the Roots to the Tree and if their minds are clean and they are obedient and promise to obey the wishes of the Confederate Council, they shall be welcomed to take shelter beneath the Tree of the Long Leaves. We place at the top of the Tree of the Long Leaves an Eagle who is able to see afar. If he sees in the distance any evil approaching or any danger threatening he will at once warn the people of the Confederacy.

. . .

Skill: Central or Main Idea

The eagle might symbolize foresight in watching out for danger. The preservation of peace seems to be an important idea of this passage.

1 Introduction

An Introduction to each text provides historical context for your reading as well as information about the author. You will also learn about the genre of the text and the year in which it was written.

2 Notes

Many times, while working through the activities after each text, you will be asked to **annotate** or **make annotations** about what you are reading. This means that you should highlight or underline words in the text and use the "Notes" column to make comments or jot down any questions you have. You may also want to note any unfamiliar vocabulary words here.

You will also see sample student annotations to go along with the Skill lesson for that text.

3 First Read

During your first reading of each selection, you should just try to get a general idea of the content and message of the reading. Don't worry if there are parts you don't understand or words that are unfamiliar to you. You'll have an opportunity later to dive deeper into the text.

4 Think Questions

These questions will ask you to start thinking critically about the text, asking specific questions about its purpose, and making connections to your prior knowledge and reading experiences. To answer these questions, you should go back to the text and draw upon specific evidence to support your responses. You will also begin to explore some of the more challenging vocabulary words in the selection.

5 Skills

Each Skill includes two parts: Checklist and Your Turn. In the Checklist, you will learn the process for analyzing the text. The model student annotations in the text provide examples of how you might make your own notes following the instructions in the Checklist. In the Your Turn, you will use those same instructions to practice the skill.

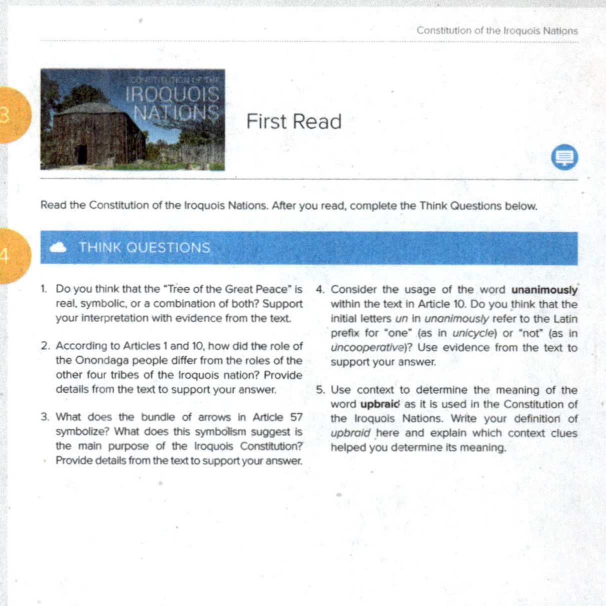

Constitution of the Iroquois Nations

3 First Read

Read the Constitution of the Iroquois Nations. After you read, complete the Think Questions below.

4 THINK QUESTIONS

1. Do you think that the "Tree of the Great Peace" is real, symbolic, or a combination of both? Support your interpretation with evidence from the text.
2. According to Articles 1 and 10, how did the role of the Onondaga people differ from the roles of the other four tribes of the Iroquois nation? Provide details from the text to support your answer.
3. What does the bundle of arrows in Article 57 symbolize? What does this symbolism suggest is the main purpose of the Iroquois Constitution? Provide details from the text to support your answer.
4. Consider the usage of the word **unanimously** within the text in Article 10. Do you think that the initial letters *un* in *unanimously* refer to the Latin prefix for "one" (as in *unicycle*) or "not" (as in *uncooperative*)? Use evidence from the text to support your answer.
5. Use context to determine the meaning of the word **upbraid** as it is used in the Constitution of the Iroquois Nations. Write your definition of *upbraid* here and explain which context clues helped you determine its meaning.

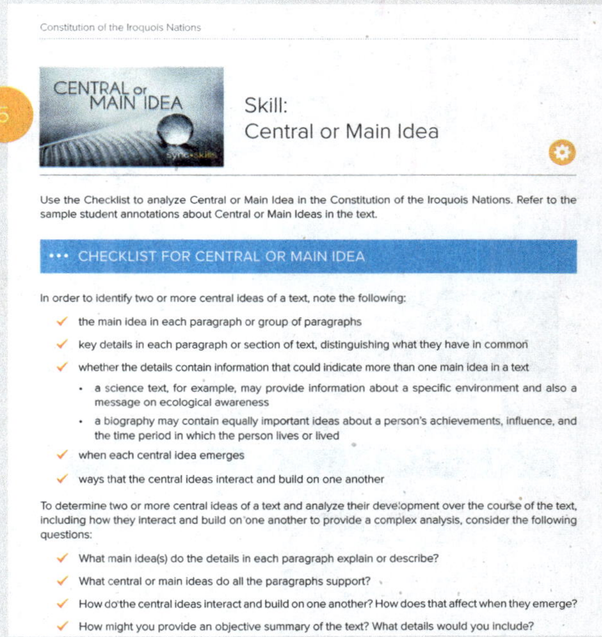

Constitution of the Iroquois Nations

5 Skill: Central or Main Idea

Use the Checklist to analyze Central or Main Idea in the Constitution of the Iroquois Nations. Refer to the sample student annotations about Central or Main Ideas in the text.

CHECKLIST FOR CENTRAL OR MAIN IDEA

In order to identify two or more central ideas of a text, note the following:

- ✓ the main idea in each paragraph or group of paragraphs
- ✓ key details in each paragraph or section of text, distinguishing what they have in common
- ✓ whether the details contain information that could indicate more than one main idea in a text
  - a science text, for example, may provide information about a specific environment and also a message on ecological awareness
  - a biography may contain equally important ideas about a person's achievements, influence, and the time period in which the person lives or lived
- ✓ when each central idea emerges
- ✓ ways that the central ideas interact and build on one another

To determine two or more central ideas of a text and analyze their development over the course of the text, including how they interact and build on one another to provide a complex analysis, consider the following questions:

- ✓ What main idea(s) do the details in each paragraph explain or describe?
- ✓ What central or main ideas do all the paragraphs support?
- ✓ How do the central ideas interact and build on one another? How does that affect when they emerge?
- ✓ How might you provide an objective summary of the text? What details would you include?

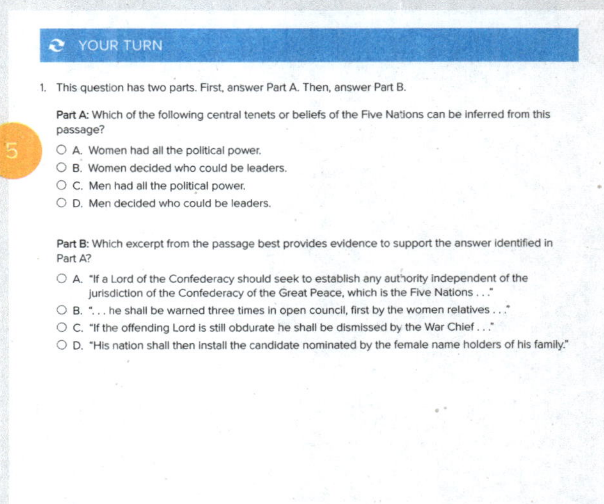

5 YOUR TURN

1. This question has two parts. First, answer Part A. Then, answer Part B.

Part A: Which of the following central tenets or beliefs of the Five Nations can be inferred from this passage?

- A. Women had all the political power.
- B. Women decided who could be leaders.
- C. Men had all the political power.
- D. Men decided who could be leaders.

Part B: Which excerpt from the passage best provides evidence to support the answer identified in Part A?

- A. "If a Lord of the Confederacy should seek to establish any authority independent of the jurisdiction of the Confederacy of the Great Peace, which is the Five Nations . . ."
- B. ". . . he shall be warned three times in open council, first by the women relatives . . ."
- C. "If the offending Lord is still obdurate he shall be dismissed by the War Chief . . ."
- D. "His nation shall then install the candidate nominated by the female name holders of his family."

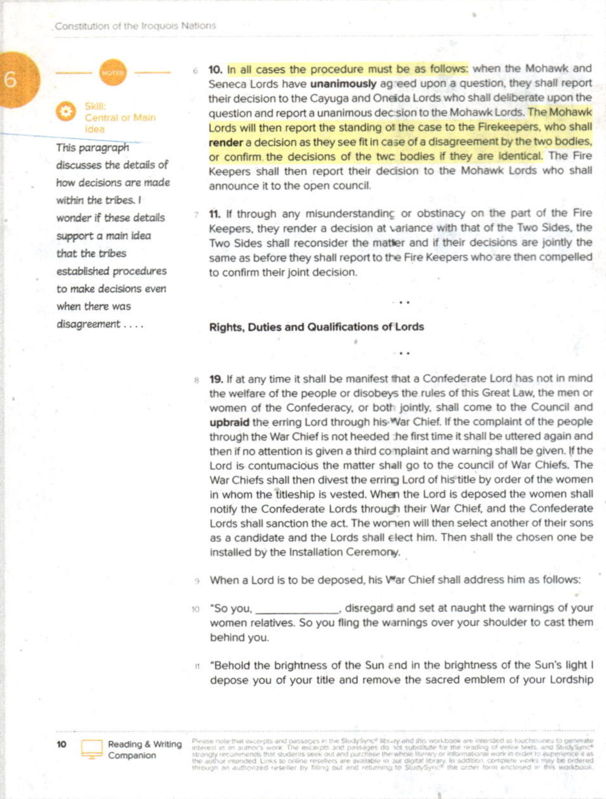
Constitution of the Iroquois Nations

6 NOTES

Skill: Central or Main Idea

This paragraph discusses the details of how decisions are made within the tribes. I wonder if these details support a main idea that the tribes established procedures to make decisions even when there was disagreement . . . .

6 **10.** In all cases the procedure must be as follows: when the Mohawk and Seneca Lords have **unanimously** agreed upon a question, they shall report their decision to the Cayuga and Oneida Lords who shall deliberate upon the question and report a unanimous decision to the Mohawk Lords. The Mohawk Lords will then report the standing of the case to the Firekeepers, who shall **render** a decision as they see fit in case of a disagreement by the two bodies, or confirm the decisions of the two bodies if they are identical. The Fire Keepers shall then report their decision to the Mohawk Lords who shall announce it to the open council.

7 **11.** If through any misunderstanding or obstinacy on the part of the Fire Keepers, they render a decision at variance with that of the Two Sides, the Two Sides shall reconsider the matter and if their decisions are jointly the same as before they shall report to the Fire Keepers who are then compelled to confirm their joint decision.

. . .

Rights, Duties and Qualifications of Lords

. . .

8 **19.** If at any time it shall be manifest that a Confederate Lord has not in mind the welfare of the people or disobeys the rules of this Great Law, the men or women of the Confederacy, or both jointly, shall come to the Council and **upbraid** the erring Lord through his War Chief. If the complaint of the people through the War Chief is not heeded the first time it shall be uttered again and then if no attention is given a third complaint and warning shall be given. If the Lord is contumacious the matter shall go to the council of War Chiefs. The War Chiefs shall then divest the erring Lord of his title by order of the women in whom the titleship is vested. When the Lord is deposed the women shall notify the Confederate Lords through their War Chief, and the Confederate Lords shall sanction the act. The women will then select another of their sons as a candidate and the Lords shall elect him. Then shall the chosen one be installed by the Installation Ceremony.

9 When a Lord is to be deposed, his War Chief shall address him as follows:

10 "So you, ____________, disregard and set at naught the warnings of your women relatives. So you fling the warnings over your shoulder to cast them behind you.

11 "Behold the brightness of the Sun and in the brightness of the Sun's light I depose you of your title and remove the sacred emblem of your Lordship

10 Reading & Writing Companion

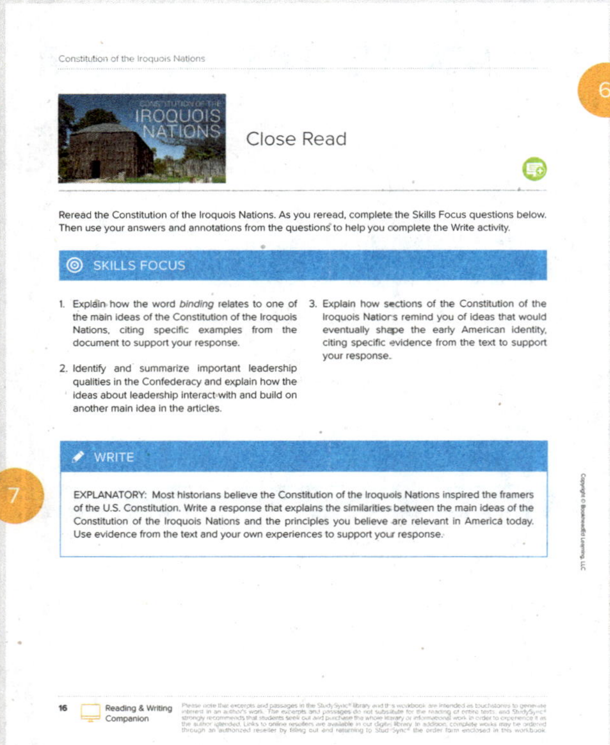
Constitution of the Iroquois Nations

CONSTITUTION OF THE IROQUOIS NATIONS

Close Read

6

Reread the Constitution of the Iroquois Nations. As you reread, complete the Skills Focus questions below. Then use your answers and annotations from the questions to help you complete the Write activity.

SKILLS FOCUS

1. Explain how the word *binding* relates to one of the main ideas of the Constitution of the Iroquois Nations, citing specific examples from the document to support your response.
2. Identify and summarize important leadership qualities in the Confederacy and explain how the ideas about leadership interact with and build on another main idea in the articles.
3. Explain how sections of the Constitution of the Iroquois Nations remind you of ideas that would eventually shape the early American identity, citing specific evidence from the text to support your response.

WRITE

7

EXPLANATORY: Most historians believe the Constitution of the Iroquois Nations inspired the framers of the U.S. Constitution. Write a response that explains the similarities between the main ideas of the Constitution of the Iroquois Nations and the principles you believe are relevant in America today. Use evidence from the text and your own experiences to support your response.

16 Reading & Writing Companion

6 Close Read & Skills Focus

After you have completed the First Read, you will be asked to go back and read the text more closely and critically. Before you begin your Close Read, you should read through the Skills Focus to get an idea of the concepts you will want to focus on during your second reading. You should work through the Skills Focus by making annotations, highlighting important concepts, and writing notes or questions in the "Notes" column. Depending on instructions from your teacher, you may need to respond online or use a separate piece of paper to start expanding on your thoughts and ideas.

7 Write

Your study of each selection will end with a writing assignment. For this assignment, you should use your notes, annotations, personal ideas, and answers to both the Think and the Skills Focus questions. Be sure to read the prompt carefully and address each part of it in your writing.

Extended Writing Project and Grammar

This is your opportunity to use genre characteristics and craft to compose meaningful, longer written works exploring the theme of each unit. You will draw information from your readings, research, and own life experiences to complete the assignment.

1 Writing Project

After you have read all of the unit text selections, you will move on to a writing project. Each project will guide you through the process of writing your essay. Student models will provide guidance and help you organize your thoughts. One unit ends with an **Extended Oral Project,** which will give you an opportunity to develop your oral language and communication skills.

2 Writing Process Steps

There are four steps in the writing process: Plan, Draft, Revise, and Edit and Publish. During each step, you will form and shape your writing project, and each lesson's peer review will give you the chance to receive feedback from your peers and teacher.

3 Writing Skills

Each Skill lesson focuses on a specific strategy or technique that you will use during your writing project. Each lesson presents a process for applying the skill to your own work and gives you the opportunity to practice it to improve your writing.

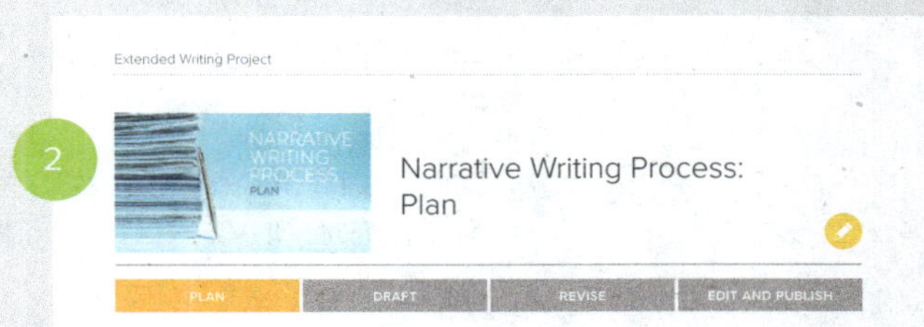

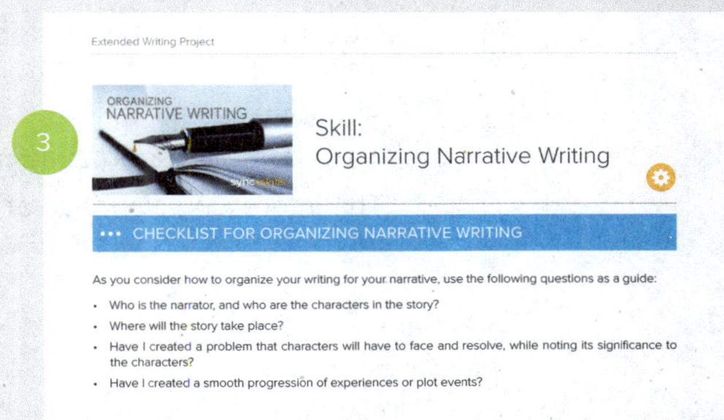

We the People

How does independence define the American spirit?

Literary Focus: **EARLY AMERICA**

Texts

PAIRED READINGS

Extended Writing Project and Grammar

Talk Back Text

Talk Back Texts are works from a later period that engage with the themes and tropes of the unit's literary focus. Demonstrating that literature is always in conversation, these texts provide dynamic new perspectives to complement the unit's more traditional chronology.

Unit 1: We the People

How does independence define the American spirit?

ABIGAIL ADAMS

Abigail Adams (1744–1818) was a descendent of the politically connected Quincy family. Taught by her mother to read and write (women generally did not receive a formal education at the time), Adams's letters reflect her lifelong advocacy for women's rights and the abolition of slavery. Much more overtly politically active than her First Lady predecessor, Martha Washington, Adams earned the nickname "Mrs. President," given her level of influence over John Adams's decisions.

MARYSE CONDÉ

Maryse Condé (b. 1937) is a French Guadeloupean writer living in New York and Guadeloupe. Her historical fiction considers gender and cultural dynamics through the lens of the diaspora, and has focused on such periods as the Salem witch trials and the building of the Panama Canal. Of her writing, Condé has said, "I could not write anything—although I write an entertaining fantasy novel—unless it has a certain political significance."

OLAUDAH EQUIANO

Olaudah Equiano's (c. 1745–1797) autobiography, *The Interesting Narrative of the Life of Olaudah Equiano, or Gustavus Vassa, the African* (1789) is one of the earliest books published by a black African writer. At a young age, Equiano was kidnapped from his home in what is now southern Nigeria and sold into slavery. He bought his own freedom in 1766 and settled in England, where he became an ardent abolitionist. His autobiography was a major contribution to the anti-slavery movement.

BENJAMIN FRANKLIN

Nicknamed "The First American," Benjamin Franklin (1706–1790) was, among other things, a writer, an inventor, a musician, a postmaster, a humorist, a diplomat, and a Founding Father. Born in Boston, Massachusetts, Franklin ran away at seventeen to Philadelphia, where he spent most of his adult life. Despite having only two years of formal education, Franklin is considered one of the most impactful figures in America's history.

NATHANIEL HAWTHORNE

Born in Salem, Massachusetts, Nathaniel Hawthorne (1804–1864) set most of his novels and short stories in colonial New England, as his ancestors had been some of its original founders. In his best-known work, *The Scarlet Letter* (1850), he scrutinizes the staunch moralism of the Puritan tradition he had inherited. Taking up the theme of guilt in the novel, Hawthorne probes his characters' psychologies and the hypocrisy of dominant social values.

THOMAS JEFFERSON

The third president of the United States, Thomas Jefferson (1743–1826) also drafted the Declaration of Independence. This foundational document, ratified on July 4, 1776, established the thirteen American British colonies' independence from Great Britain. In writing the text, Jefferson drew on political philosopher John Locke's theory of "natural law," which suggested that human beings are "by nature free, equal and independent." Jefferson was a staunch advocate of individual freedom, which he considered to be a key tenet of the American Revolution.

DAVID MCCULLOUGH

Originally from Philadelphia, David McCullough (b. 1933) is a narrative historian who most frequently writes about key moments and figures in American history. After the publication of his first book, *The Johnstown Flood*, McCullough received offers to write about historical disasters (he declined, not wanting to be known as "Bad News McCullough"). Reflected in his work is McCullough's belief that "History is the story of people."

ARTHUR MILLER

Playwright, essayist, and husband of four years to Marilyn Monroe, Arthur Miller (1915–2005) was the son of Polish Jewish immigrants and grew up in New York City. Miller's work frequently explores social conscience and family dynamics. He was famously outspoken in his opposition to Joseph McCarthy's allegations of communist infiltration into the United States, which Miller allegorically likened to the Salem witch trials in his play, *The Crucible*.

PHILLIS WHEATLEY

Phillis Wheatley's (1753–1784) *Poems on Various Subjects, Religious and Moral* (1773) was the first volume of poetry by an African American published in modern times. Wheatley was brought to the United States from West Africa in 1761 and ended up in Boston as an enslaved person in the home of the Wheatley family. Like much of her work, her best-known poem, "On Being Brought from Africa to America," uses biblical symbolism to comment on slavery. Wheatley may have written as many as 145 poems, most of which are now lost.

WILLIAM BRADFORD

Born in Northern England, William Bradford (1590–1657) came to Plymouth Colony by way of the *Mayflower* in a series of moves to escape religious persecution from King James I. A meticulous record keeper, Bradford even transcribed the Mayflower Compact into his journal. His is one of only three remaining copies from the 17th century. Bradford's most famous work, *Of Plymouth Plantation*, documents three decades in the early years of Plymouth Colony and is considered the preeminent historical record of America from the period.

ANNE BRADSTREET

Anne Bradstreet (c. 1612–1672) immigrated to America from England at the age of eighteen with her husband and parents to join the Puritans at the Massachusetts Bay Colony. They were met with distressing conditions, such as sickness and food scarcity, when they arrived but settled there regardless. Bradstreet returned to the theme of women in Puritan society throughout her many volumes of poetry. She became the first published American poet when her brother-in-law had some of her poems published in England in 1650 without her knowledge.

JUPITER HAMMON

The first African American poet published in the United States, Jupiter Hammon (1711–c. 1806) was a devout Christian born into slavery in New York. His second poem, a direct address to Phillis Wheatley, expressed the controversial opinion that it was through the mercy of the Lord that she had left "the heathen shore" and entreated her to better herself in the eyes of God. Hammon was never emancipated, though he supported the abolitionist movement.

DEKANAWIDAH

Dekanawidah, known as the Great Peace Maker, united five Iroquois nations torn apart by fighting in present-day New York to form the Iroquois Confederacy, now considered to be one of the world's oldest participator democracies. Dekanawidah's name, meaning "Two River Currents Flowing Together," symbolizes the peacemaking legacy for which he is remembered. Along with his spokesman Hiawatha, he formulated the Great Law of Peace, the oral constitution of the Iroquois Confederacy originally written on wampum belts before being translated into English.

LITERARY FOCUS:

Early America

Introduction

This informational text offers background about the history and culture that defined early American literature, including written and oral pieces from indigenous, European, and African voices. Readers will explore early, groundbreaking literature about self-government and consider the progressive ideals of the time, which influenced its most memorable works. What great texts, for example, inspired America's foundational documents? Amidst the different religious and philosophical movements of their respective times, works like the Constitution of the Iroquois Nations and the Declaration of Independence set the framework for a new democracy.

". . . new, never-before-seen ideas emerge from the interactions of diverse cultures."

NOTES

1 American culture is characterized by its blend of features from other cultures. Barbecue, for example, is based upon on a native Caribbean cooking technique, uses European ingredients, and was popularized and spread by African Americans. Jazz and blues make use of European-inspired harmonies and African-inspired rhythms. In many aspects of American life, you can find influences from the cultures of Native Americans, European colonists, and Africans. Even the earliest examples of American literature show how new, never-before-seen ideas emerge from the interactions of diverse cultures.

The First Peoples

2 Between about 40,000 and 10,000 BCE, small bands of people crossed a land bridge between Asia and North America—where the Bering Strait exists today—and began to settle in North America. Over time, the population grew and spread to form hundreds of diverse indigenous cultures in North and South America. For thousands of years, the cultures of indigenous peoples of North America flourished. Some societies developed writing systems, especially those in modern-day Mexico and Central America, but the majority of Native American peoples maintained a rich oral literature tradition to preserve their beliefs and histories. The Constitution of the Iroquois Nations, which contained some of the original ideas about **self-government** and later influenced the creation of the founding documents of the United States of America, was passed down for hundreds of years through Native American oral traditions.

Painting by Henry Bruckner (ca. 1855) depicting the marriage of British colonist John Rolfe to Pocahontas, the daughter of Chief Powhatan of the Algonquian tribe, in 1614

NOTES

Colonization

3 The existence of North and South America was largely unknown to Europeans until the voyages of Christopher Columbus in the late fifteenth century brought widespread attention to the region. In the ensuing rush to gain economic and territorial power, Spain, England, and other countries began to establish **colonies** in what Amerigo Vespucci called *Mundus Novus*, or the New World.

4 Initial accounts from early colonists told stories of a land rich in resources and opportunity, compelling people from all over Europe to cross the Atlantic to seek a new life in North America.

5 When the early settlers arrived, they began interacting with the indigenous peoples who had long inhabited the land. The desire of European settlers to claim physical territory and establish colonial culture often resulted in widespread violence against Native Americans. This oppression of others was also spurred by a desire for economic gain. For example, as early as 1501, the Spanish started kidnapping and enslaving Africans, forcibly bringing them from their native continent to the Americas as part of a widespread slave trade that was both extremely profitable and inhumane.

6 What resulted was a society of people from wide-ranging backgrounds, comprised of the oppressed and the oppressors, all speaking a multitude of languages, including Spanish, English, German, Portuguese, Dutch, French, a variety of African languages, and, of course, indigenous languages. The tumultuous, and at times violent, interaction of these diverse cultures in North America during the early colonial period contributed to the formation of a unique and fraught American cultural identity.

7 Eventually, as England colonized the entire Eastern Seaboard north of Florida, English became the most common language and literature in the colonies. Much of the literature the colonists read and drew from in their own writings originated in Britain. England had a well-established literary tradition at the time—Shakespeare had died only four years before the Pilgrims landed at Plymouth in 1620. By contrast, because North American settlers were occupied with establishing the colonies and had little time to devote to the creation of original works of fiction, the majority of early colonial literature was utilitarian—observations of North American geography, biographies, and treatises. There was also a significant body of religious literature because many of the English colonists were Puritans who had come to North America seeking religious freedom. **Puritanism** was a religious movement of Reformed Protestants who felt that the Church of England, which had split from the Roman Catholic Church in 1534, was still too similar to Catholicism and needed further reform. While colonial literature was still heavily influenced by the

NOTES

English, the Puritans' efforts to differentiate themselves from English religious culture had a strong influence on new ideas that had begun to percolate in the colonial imagination.

8 In the eighteenth century, two important movements had a defining influence on colonial culture: the **Enlightenment** and the **Great Awakening**. The Enlightenment was a philosophical movement that promoted the use of reason in all areas of intellectual life. Enlightenment ideas swept through the entire Western world and had revolutionary effects on both sides of the Atlantic. European Enlightenment philosophers, including John Locke and Thomas Hobbes, introduced a political philosophy concerned with equality and the natural rights of man, which provided a foundation for the creation of modern democracies. In North America, Benjamin Franklin, Thomas Paine, and Thomas Jefferson incorporated Enlightenment ideas into their rhetoric, urging the Thirteen British Colonies to break their ties to England and eventually leading to the **Revolutionary War** and the Declaration of Independence.

9 What's more, in the 1730s and 1740s, a growing religious movement, known as the Great Awakening, began to gain popularity in the colonies. Reform Protestants, like George Whitefield and Jonathan Edwards, preached to large groups about a more personal approach to faith and successfully converted large numbers of people from a variety of religious, social, and racial backgrounds. Both the Enlightenment and the Great Awakening helped to shape a distinctively American sense of identity, encouraging people to find their own way rather than subject themselves to the power of traditional governments and religious institutions. In the process of intellectual exploration and debate, the colonists ultimately formulated dramatic new ideas about reason, religion, and independence that led to the founding of the United States of America and changed the world.

10 **Major Concepts**

- **The Sacred Earth and the Power of Storytelling** — The oral literature of Native American peoples reflected the deep connection to the earth that was at the heart of their belief system. Some stories had practical functions, such as helping to keep track of seasons, animal migrations, harvest times, and other periodic phenomena, but other narratives had a more spiritual purpose. Creation myths described how the earth began, and origin myths explained how things like the moon or mountains were made. Many stories emphasized the sacred harmony, or interdependence, between humans and the natural world.

- **Life in the New World** — Many of the inhabitants of North America during the colonial period were struggling to adapt to unfamiliar circumstances. Native Americans saw the land they had inhabited for thousands of years overrun by newcomers; they saw their populations being decimated by

NOTES

European diseases and colonization, which culminated in violent battles over territory. Early European settlers sought to establish themselves and tame what they viewed as a wild and alien environment, documenting their efforts in diaries, letters, and books. Enslaved Africans passed on oral and written accounts of their daily struggle to survive the violence and degradation imposed on them by colonial masters.

- **The Road to Independence** — In order to fund the Seven Years' War with France, Great Britain imposed high taxes on the colonists. They also sent soldiers to the colonies to enforce regulations and maintain control of the territory. Without representation in the British Parliament—England's legislative body—colonists had no power to voice their opposition to the taxes and policies imposed on them. The colonists shared the view of Enlightenment philosophers who believed that a government's authority was dependent upon the consent of the governed. Literature of the late colonial period dealt with these conflicts, as well as with ideas of justice, independence, and how to create a better society.

John Trumbull's 1818 painting depicting the presentation of the Declaration of Independence to Congress in 1776

Style and Form

11 **Native American Literature**

- Native American oral literature incorporated pattern, repetition, and structural formulas as mnemonic devices, or memory aids. How these elements were used in a given story influenced the story's style and form.
- Native American oral literature was comprised of many genres, including creation and origin myths, prayers, songs, folktales, and narratives of heroism and transformation.
- Native American oral literature was performed, not read. Thus, the translation of indigenous stories into written English sometimes caused certain aspects of the stories to be lost or recorded in a different form than how they were originally performed.

NOTES

12 Puritans

- William Bradford was a Puritan who served as governor of the Plymouth colony for over thirty years. His *Of Plymouth Plantation* provides insight into colonial life. He defined Puritan style as a "plain style, with singular regard unto the simple truth in all things."
- This plain, simple, truthful style was employed first by the Puritans but became a hallmark of early American literature. For instance, Jonathan Edwards and George Whitefield used it in their sermons.

13 Significance of Rhetoric and Rhetorical Devices

- Rhetoric is the art of speaking and writing persuasively. Classical rhetoric uses three types of appeals: *logos*, an appeal to logic; *pathos*, an emotional appeal to the audience; and *ethos*, an appeal based upon the author's expertise. Revolutionaries like Thomas Paine and Thomas Jefferson expertly adopted these rhetorical methods in their speeches and writings, most famously in Paine's *Common Sense* and in the Declaration of Independence, which was drafted by Jefferson.
- Authors use rhetorical devices like similes, metaphors, and irony, among a long list of other things, to convince their audiences in more subtle ways. Thomas Jefferson was a learned student of literature and philosophy and had a keen sense of how to use these devices. In the Declaration of Independence, he employed a straightforward style but used rhetorical devices such as alliteration, allusion, euphony, and repetition to drive home his points. The rhetoric used during the late colonial period was instrumental in fostering the revolutionary spirit that defined the times and formed the basis of the arguments that led to the founding of the United States of America.

Phillis Wheatley

NOTES

14 **Biblical Symbolism, Neoclassical Couplets, and Iambic Pentameter**

- Early American poets, such as the enslaved poet, Phillis Wheatley, sometimes took inspiration from English writers such as Alexander Pope. Neoclassical poetry, like Pope's, often used the heroic couplet. Couplets are two successive lines in which the last words rhyme. Heroic couplets are couplets written in iambic pentameter, a poetic meter with five beats, or stressed syllables.
- Biblical symbolism also appears in poems written in the period. For example, in Wheatley's "On Being Brought from Africa to America," she compares Africans to the biblical figure Cain, to whom God showed mercy.

15 Early American literature was influenced by a variety of cultures and traditions, but it also incorporated new ideas and interpreted them in a uniquely American way. People from diverse backgrounds built a new culture that was based on a foundation of Old World literary custom and invigorated by the exploration and adoption of new ideas. Combining ideas to create something new continues to fuel America's gift for innovation. Where else in modern-day America can you recognize the concepts and ideas that defined early American literature? How do diverse opinions about the guiding principles of early American culture—reason, religious freedom, and independence—continue to shape America today?

Literary Focus: Early America

Read "Literary Focus: Early America." After you read, complete the Think Questions below.

THINK QUESTIONS

1. Explain how rhetoric can be used to convince an audience. Provide examples of early American literature in which the authors utilize rhetoric. Be sure to cite evidence directly from the text.

2. What are some of the cultural differences among the various groups that inhabited the early American colonies, and how are these differences reflected in their literature? Explain, citing evidence from the text to support your response.

3. What effect did religion have on different works of early American literature? Cite evidence from the text to support your explanations.

4. Use context clues to determine the meaning of the word **colonies**. Write your best definition here, along with the words and phrases that were most helpful in determining the word's meaning. Then, check a dictionary to confirm your understanding.

5. The word **puritanism** likely stems from the Latin *puritas*, meaning "purity." With this information in mind along with context from the text, write your best definition of the word *puritanism* as it used in this text. Cite any words or phrases that were particularly helpful in coming to your conclusion.

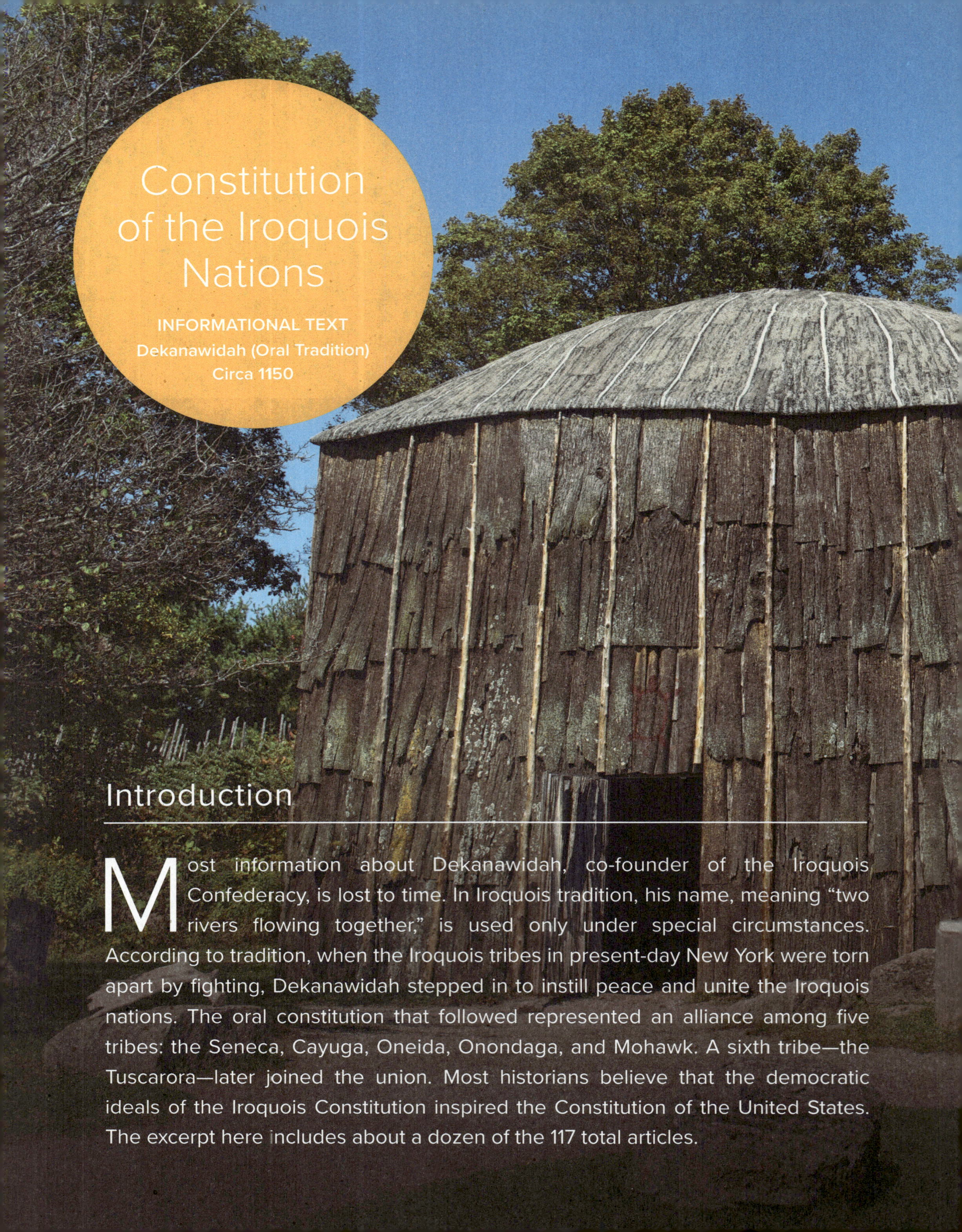

Constitution of the Iroquois Nations

INFORMATIONAL TEXT
Dekanawidah (Oral Tradition)
Circa 1150

Introduction

Most information about Dekanawidah, co-founder of the Iroquois Confederacy, is lost to time. In Iroquois tradition, his name, meaning "two rivers flowing together," is used only under special circumstances. According to tradition, when the Iroquois tribes in present-day New York were torn apart by fighting, Dekanawidah stepped in to instill peace and unite the Iroquois nations. The oral constitution that followed represented an alliance among five tribes: the Seneca, Cayuga, Oneida, Onondaga, and Mohawk. A sixth tribe—the Tuscarora—later joined the union. Most historians believe that the democratic ideals of the Iroquois Constitution inspired the Constitution of the United States. The excerpt here includes about a dozen of the 117 total articles.

"I am Dekanawidah and with the Five Nations' Confederate Lords I plant the Tree of Great Peace."

NOTES

The Great Binding Law, Gayanashagowa

1 **1.** I am Dekanawidah and with the Five Nations' Confederate Lords I plant the Tree of Great Peace. I plant it in your territory, Adodarhoh, and the Onondaga Nation, in the territory of you who are Firekeepers.

2 I name the tree the Tree of the Great Long Leaves. Under the shade of this Tree of the Great Peace we spread the soft white feathery down of the globe thistle as seats for you, Adodarhoh, and your cousin Lords.

3 We place you upon those seats, spread soft with the feathery down of the globe thistle, there beneath the shade of the spreading branches of the Tree of Peace. There shall you sit and watch the Council Fire of the Confederacy of the Five Nations, and all the affairs of the Five Nations shall be transacted at this place before you, Adodarhoh, and your cousin Lords, by the Confederate Lords of the Five Nations.

4 **2.** Roots have spread out from the Tree of the Great Peace, one to the north, one to the east, one to the south and one to the west. The name of these roots is The Great White Roots and their nature is Peace and Strength.

5 If any man or any nation outside the Five Nations shall obey the laws of the Great Peace and make known their **disposition** to the Lords of the Confederacy, they may trace the Roots to the Tree and if their minds are clean and they are obedient and promise to obey the wishes of the Confederate Council, they shall be welcomed to take shelter beneath the Tree of the Long Leaves. We place at the top of the Tree of the Long Leaves an Eagle who is able to see afar. If he sees in the distance any evil approaching or any danger threatening he will at once warn the people of the Confederacy.

. . .

Skill: Central or Main Idea

The eagle might symbolize foresight in watching out for danger. The preservation of peace seems to be an important idea of this passage.

NOTES

Skill: Central or Main Idea

This paragraph discusses the details of how decisions are made within the tribes. I wonder if these details support a main idea that the tribes established procedures to make decisions even when there was disagreement . . . .

6 **10.** In all cases the procedure must be as follows: when the Mohawk and Seneca Lords have **unanimously** agreed upon a question, they shall report their decision to the Cayuga and Oneida Lords who shall deliberate upon the question and report a unanimous decision to the Mohawk Lords. The Mohawk Lords will then report the standing of the case to the Firekeepers, who shall **render** a decision as they see fit in case of a disagreement by the two bodies, or confirm the decisions of the two bodies if they are identical. The Fire Keepers shall then report their decision to the Mohawk Lords who shall announce it to the open council.

7 **11.** If through any misunderstanding or obstinacy on the part of the Fire Keepers, they render a decision at variance with that of the Two Sides, the Two Sides shall reconsider the matter and if their decisions are jointly the same as before they shall report to the Fire Keepers who are then compelled to confirm their joint decision.

. . .

Rights, Duties and Qualifications of Lords

. . .

8 **19.** If at any time it shall be manifest that a Confederate Lord has not in mind the welfare of the people or disobeys the rules of this Great Law, the men or women of the Confederacy, or both jointly, shall come to the Council and **upbraid** the erring Lord through his War Chief. If the complaint of the people through the War Chief is not heeded the first time it shall be uttered again and then if no attention is given a third complaint and warning shall be given. If the Lord is contumacious the matter shall go to the council of War Chiefs. The War Chiefs shall then divest the erring Lord of his title by order of the women in whom the titleship is vested. When the Lord is deposed the women shall notify the Confederate Lords through their War Chief, and the Confederate Lords shall sanction the act. The women will then select another of their sons as a candidate and the Lords shall elect him. Then shall the chosen one be installed by the Installation Ceremony.

9 When a Lord is to be deposed, his War Chief shall address him as follows:

10 "So you, ______________, disregard and set at naught the warnings of your women relatives. So you fling the warnings over your shoulder to cast them behind you.

11 "Behold the brightness of the Sun and in the brightness of the Sun's light I depose you of your title and remove the sacred emblem of your Lordship

NOTES

title. I remove from your brow the deer's antlers, which was the emblem of your position and token of your nobility. I now depose you and return the antlers to the women whose heritage they are."

• • •

12 **25.** If a Lord of the Confederacy should seek to establish any authority independent of the jurisdiction of the Confederacy of the Great Peace, which is the Five Nations, he shall be warned three times in open council, first by the women relatives, second by the men relatives and finally by the Lords of the Confederacy of the Nation to which he belongs. If the offending Lord is still obdurate he shall be dismissed by the War Chief of his nation for refusing to conform to the laws of the Great Peace. His nation shall then install the candidate nominated by the female name holders of his family.

13 **26.** It shall be the duty of all of the Five Nations Confederate Lords, from time to time as occasion demands, to act as mentors and spiritual guides of their people and remind them of their Creator's will and words. They shall say:

14 "Hearken, that peace may continue unto future days! "Always listen to the words of the Great Creator, for he has spoken. "United people, let not evil find lodging in your minds. "For the Great Creator has spoken and the cause of Peace shall not become old. "The cause of peace shall not die if you remember the Great Creator." Every Confederate Lord shall speak words such as these to promote peace.

15 **27.** All Lords of the Five Nations Confederacy must be honest in all things. They must not idle or gossip, but be men possessing those honorable qualities that make true royaneh. It shall be a serious wrong for anyone to lead a Lord into trivial affairs, for the people must ever hold their Lords high in estimation out of respect to their honorable positions.

• • •

Names, Duties and Rights of War Chiefs

• • •

16 **37.** There shall be one War Chief for each Nation and their duties shall be to carry messages for their Lords and to take up the arms of war in case of emergency. They shall not participate in the proceedings of the Confederate Council but shall watch its progress and in case of an erroneous action by a Lord they shall receive the complaints of the people and **convey** the warnings of the women to him. The people who wish to convey messages to the Lords

NOTES

in the Confederate Council shall do so through the War Chief of their Nation. It shall ever be his duty to lay the cases, questions and propositions of the people before the Confederate Council.

. . .

Official Symbolism

. . .

17 **57.** Five arrows shall be bound together very strong and each arrow shall represent one nation. As the five arrows are strongly bound this shall symbolize the complete union of the nations. Thus are the Five Nations united completely and enfolded together, united into one head, one body and one mind. Therefore they shall labor, legislate and council together for the interest of future generations. The Lords of the Confederacy shall eat together from one bowl the feast of cooked beaver's tail. While they are eating they are to use no sharp utensils for if they should they might accidentally cut one another and bloodshed would follow. All measures must be taken to prevent the spilling of blood in any way.

. . .

Religious Ceremonies Protected

18 **99.** The rites and festivals of each nation shall remain undisturbed and shall continue as before because they were given by the people of old times as useful and necessary for the good of men.

First Read

Read the Constitution of the Iroquois Nations. After you read, complete the Think Questions below.

THINK QUESTIONS

1. Do you think that the "Tree of the Great Peace" is real, symbolic, or a combination of both? Support your interpretation with evidence from the text.

2. According to Articles 1 and 10, how did the role of the Onondaga people differ from the roles of the other four tribes of the Iroquois nation? Provide details from the text to support your answer.

3. What does the bundle of arrows in Article 57 symbolize? What does this symbolism suggest is the main purpose of the Iroquois Constitution? Provide details from the text to support your answer.

4. Consider the usage of the word **unanimously** within the text in Article 10. Do you think that the initial letters *un* in *unanimously* refer to the Latin prefix for "one" (as in *unicycle*) or "not" (as in *uncooperative*)? Use evidence from the text to support your answer.

5. Use context to determine the meaning of the word **upbraid** as it is used in the Constitution of the Iroquois Nations. Write your definition of *upbraid* here and explain which context clues helped you determine its meaning.

Skill: Central or Main Idea

Use the Checklist to analyze Central or Main Idea in the Constitution of the Iroquois Nations. Refer to the sample student annotations about Central or Main Ideas in the text.

••• CHECKLIST FOR CENTRAL OR MAIN IDEA

In order to identify two or more central ideas of a text, note the following:

- ✓ the main idea in each paragraph or group of paragraphs
- ✓ key details in each paragraph or section of text, distinguishing what they have in common
- ✓ whether the details contain information that could indicate more than one main idea in a text
  - a science text, for example, may provide information about a specific environment and also a message on ecological awareness
  - a biography may contain equally important ideas about a person's achievements, influence, and the time period in which the person lives or lived
- ✓ when each central idea emerges
- ✓ ways that the central ideas interact and build on one another

To determine two or more central ideas of a text and analyze their development over the course of the text, including how they interact and build on one another to provide a complex analysis, consider the following questions:

- ✓ What main idea(s) do the details in each paragraph explain or describe?
- ✓ What central or main ideas do all the paragraphs support?
- ✓ How do the central ideas interact and build on one another? How does that affect when they emerge?
- ✓ How might you provide an objective summary of the text? What details would you include?

Skill: Central or Main Idea

Reread Article 25 of the Constitution of the Iroquois Nations. Then, using the Checklist on the previous page, answer the multiple-choice questions below.

YOUR TURN

1. This question has two parts. First, answer Part A. Then, answer Part B.

   Part A: Which of the following central tenets or beliefs of the Five Nations can be inferred from this passage?

   - A. Women had all the political power.
   - B. Women decided who could be leaders.
   - C. Men had all the political power.
   - D. Men decided who could be leaders.

   Part B: Which excerpt from the passage best provides evidence to support the answer identified in Part A?

   - A. "If a Lord of the Confederacy should seek to establish any authority independent of the jurisdiction of the Confederacy of the Great Peace, which is the Five Nations . . ."
   - B. ". . . he shall be warned three times in open council, first by the women relatives . . ."
   - C. "If the offending Lord is still obdurate he shall be dismissed by the War Chief . . ."
   - D. "His nation shall then install the candidate nominated by the female name holders of his family."

Close Read

Reread the Constitution of the Iroquois Nations. As you reread, complete the Skills Focus questions below. Then use your answers and annotations from the questions to help you complete the Write activity.

SKILLS FOCUS

1. Explain how the word *binding* relates to one of the main ideas of the Constitution of the Iroquois Nations, citing specific examples from the document to support your response.
2. Identify and summarize important leadership qualities in the Confederacy and explain how the ideas about leadership interact with and build on another main idea in the articles.
3. Explain how sections of the Constitution of the Iroquois Nations remind you of ideas that would eventually shape the early American identity, citing specific evidence from the text to support your response.

WRITE

EXPLANATORY: Most historians believe the Constitution of the Iroquois Nations inspired the framers of the U.S. Constitution. Write a response that explains the similarities between the main ideas of the Constitution of the Iroquois Nations and the principles you believe are relevant in America today. Use evidence from the text and your own experiences to support your response.

Of Plymouth Plantation

INFORMATIONAL TEXT
William Bradford
1630–1651

Introduction

In December of 1620, about 100 settlers disembarked the *Mayflower* near a site they named Plymouth, after the town in England where they had set sail. They were Puritan Separatists, a religious group looking to break away from the Church of England and find religious freedom in the Americas. Now known as the Pilgrims, the colonists arrived at the onset of winter, with little food and no wilderness survival skills. Though nearly half died of scurvy, pneumonia, fever, or starvation, the colony survived, and under William Bradford's leadership grew into a thriving community. In 1630, Bradford (1590–1657) began writing *Of Plymouth Plantation, 1620–1647,* which exists today as the most complete story of the Pilgrims.

"Being thus arrived in a good harbor and brought safe to land . . ."

NOTES

from Chapter 9: Of Their Voyage, & How They Passed the Sea, and of Their Safe Arrival at Cape Cod (September 1620)

1 In sundry of these storms the winds were so fierce, & the seas so high, as they could not bear a knot of sail, but were forced to hull, for diverse days together. And in one of them, as they thus lay at hull, in a mighty storm, a lusty young man (called John Howland) coming upon some occasion above the gratings, was, with a seele of the ship, thrown into the sea; but it pleased God that he caught hold of the top-sail halliards, which hung overboard & ran out at length; yet he held his hold (though he was sundry fathoms under water) till he was hauled up by the same rope to the brim of the water, and then with a boat hook & other means got into the ship again, & his life saved; and though he was something ill with it, yet he lived many years after, and became a profitable member both in church & commonwealth. In all this voyage there died but one of the passengers, which was William Butten, a youth, servant to Samuel Fuller, when they drew near the coast. . . .

2 Being thus arrived in a good harbor and brought safe to land, they fell upon their knees & blessed the God of heaven, who had brought them over the vast & furious ocean, and delivered them from all the perils & miseries thereof, again to set their feet on the firm and stable earth, their proper element. And no marvel if they were thus joyful, seeing wise Seneca[1] was so affected with sailing a few miles on the coast of his owne Italy; as he affirmed, that he had rather remained twenty years on his way by land, then pass by sea to any place in a short time; so **tedious** & dreadful was the same unto him.

3 But here I cannot but stay and make a pause, and stand half amazed at this poor people's present condition; and so I think will the reader too, when he well considers the same. Being thus passed the vast ocean, and a sea of troubles before in their preparation (as may be remembered by yet which went before), they had now no friends to welcome them, nor inns to entertain or refresh their weatherbeaten bodys, no houses or much less towns to repair too, to seek for succor. It is recorded in scripture as a mercy to the

1. **Seneca** Stoic philosopher and rhetorician; a famous philosopher who tutored many prominent people in Rome, including the Emperor Nero.

NOTES

apostle[2] & his shipwrecked company, yet the barbarians showed them no small kindness in refreshing them, but these savage barbarians, when they met with them (as after will appear) were readier to fill their sides full of arrows then otherwise. And for the season it was winter, and they that know the winters of that country know them to be sharp & violent, & subject to cruel & fierce storms, dangerous to travel to known places, much more to search an unknown coast. . . .

from the Second Book (Winter, 1620–1621)

4 But that which was most sad & lamentable was, that in two or three months time half of their company died, especially in January & February, being the depth of winter, and wanting houses & other comforts; being infected with the scurvy & other diseases, which this long voyage & their inaccommodate condition had brought upon them; so as there died some times two or three of a day, in the foresaid time; that of 100 & odd persons, scarce fifty remained. And of these in the time of most distress, there was but six or seven sound persons, who, to their great commendations be it spoken, spared no pains, night nor day, but with **abundance** of toil and hazard of their own health, fetched them wood, made them fires, dressed them meat, made their beads, washed their loathsome clothes, cloathed & uncloathed them; in a word, did all the homely & necessary offices for them which dainty & queasy stomachs cannot endure to hear named; and all this willingly & cheerfully, without any grudging in the least, showing herein their true love unto their friends & brethren. A rare example & worthy to be remembered. Two of these seven were Mr. William Brewster, their reverend Elder, & Myles Standish, their Captain & military commander, unto whom my self, & many others, were much beholden in our low & sick condition. And yet the Lord so upheld these persons, as in this general calamity they were not at all infected either with sickness, or lameness. . . .

5 All this while the Indians[3] came skulking about them, and would sometimes show themselves **aloof** of, but when any approached near them, they would run away. And once they stole away their tools where they had been at work, & were gone to dinner. But about the 16th of March a certain Indian came boldly amongst them, and spoke to them in broken English, which they could well understand, but marvelled at it. At length they understood by discourse with him, that he was not of these parts, but belonged to the eastern parts, where some English-ships came to fish, with whom he was acquainted, & could name sundry of them by their names, amongst whom he had got his

2. **apostle** an allusion to Paul the Apostle, who was shipwrecked on the island of Malta en route to his trial in Rome
3. **Indians** a misnomer used by Europeans to refer to Native American or Indigenous American people, originating from mistaken beliefs that Christopher Columbus had arrived in India when he landed in Antilles

NOTES

language. He became profitable to them in acquainting them with many things concerning the state of the country in the east-parts where he lived, which was afterwards profitable unto them; as also of the people here, of their names, number, & strength; of their situation & distance from this place, and who was chief amongst them. His name was Samoset; he told them also of another Indian whose name was Squanto, a native of this place, who had been in England & could speak better English than himself. Being, after some time of entertainment & gifts, dismissed, a while after he came again, & five more with him, & they brought again all ye tools that were stolen away before, and made way for the coming of their great Sachem, called Massasoyt; who, about four or five. days after, came with the chief of his friends & other attendance, with the aforesaid Squanto. With whom, after friendly entertainment, & some gifts given him, they made a peace with him (which hath now continued this twenty-four years) in these terms.

6 1. That neither he nor any of his, should injure or do hurt to any of their people.

7 2. That if any of his did any hurt to any of theirs, he should send the offender, that they might punish him.

8 3. That if anything were taken away from any of theirs, he should cause it to be restored; and they should do the like to his.

9 4. If any did unjustly war against him, they would aid him; if any did war against them, he should aid them.

10 5. He should send to his neighbors confederate, to certify them of this, that they might not wrong them, but might be likewise comprised in the conditions of peace.

11 6. That when their men came to them, they should leave their bows & arrows behind them.

12 After these things he returned to his place called Sowams, some forty miles from this place, but Squanto continued with them, and was their interpreter, and was a special instrument sent of God for their good beyond their expectation. He directed them how to set their corn, where to take fish, and to **procure** other commodities, and was also their pilot to bring them to unknown places for their profit, and never left them till he died. . . .

13 They began now to gather in the small harvest they had, and to fit up their houses and dwellings against winter, being all well recovered in health & strength, and had all things in good plenty; for as some were thus employed in affairs abroad, others were exercised in fishing, about cod, & bass, & other fish, of which they took good store, of which every family had their portion. All the

NOTES

summer there was no want. And now began to come in store of fowl, as winter approached, of which this place did abound when they came first (but afterward decreased by degrees). And besides water fowl, there was great store of wild turkeys, of which they took many, besides venison. Besides they had about a peck of meal a week to a person, or now since harvest, Indian corn to that proportion. Which made many afterwards write so largely of their plenty here to their friends in England, which were not **feigned**, but true reports.

WRITE

EXPLANATORY: Consider the perspective of another person Bradford would have encountered as Plymouth was being established. It can be someone who is mentioned in his account or someone who is not. Conduct informal research to write a response about their experience of Plymouth in the early 1600s.

Verses upon the Burning of Our House

POETRY

Anne Bradstreet

1666

Introduction

Anne Bradstreet (1612–1672) was born in England but emigrated to America at age 18 to join the Puritans at the Massachusetts Bay Colony. Her "Verses upon the Burning of Our House" describes a real-life event: in 1666, her family's home actually did burn down, destroying most of their earthly possessions. Her faith in God, however, impelled her to see this great loss as part of a larger purpose. Bradstreet wrote volumes of poetry during her life, much of it reflecting her views on the roles of women in Puritan society. She was the first female poet to be published on both sides of the Atlantic, though her writing was not without controversy—especially among those who believed that writing was not an acceptable pursuit for women.

"And piteous shrieks of dreadful voice. That fearful sound of 'Fire' and 'Fire' . . . "

NOTES

In silent night when rest I took,
For sorrow near I did not look,
I wakened was with thundering noise
And piteous shrieks of dreadful voice.
That fearful sound of "Fire" and "Fire,"
Let no man know, is my desire.
I, starting up, the light did spy,
And to my God my heart did cry
To strengthen me in my distress,
And not to leave me succorless.
Then coming out, behold a space
The flame **consume** my dwelling place.
And when I could no longer look,
I blest His name that gave and took,
That laid my goods now in the dust;
Yea, so it was, and so 'twas just.
It was His own; it was not mine.
Far be it that I should repine.
He might of all justly bereft,
But yet **sufficient** for us left.
When by the ruins oft I passed
My sorrowing eyes aside did cast
And here and there the places spy
Where oft I sat and long did lie.
Here stood that trunk, and there that chest;
There lay that store I counted best,
My pleasant things in ashes lie,
And them behold no more shall I.
Under thy roof no guest shall sit,
Nor at thy table eat a bit;
No pleasant tale shall e'er be told,
Nor things recounted done of old;
No candle e'er shall shine in thee,
Nor bridegroom's voice e'er heard shall be.

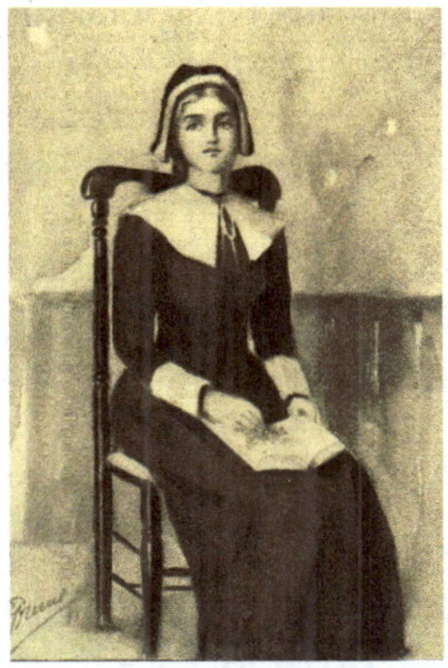

Sunday afternoon in Puritan days

NOTES

In silence ever shall thou lie.
Adieu, Adieu, all's vanity.
Then straight I 'gin my heart to **chide**:
And did thy wealth on earth abide?
Didst fix thy hope on mould'ring dust?
The arm of flesh didst make thy trust?
Raise up thy thoughts above the sky
That dunghill mists away may fly.
Thou hast a house on high erect;
Framed by that mighty Architect,
With glory richly furnishéd
Stands permanent though this be fled.
It's purchased, and paid for, too,
By him who hath enough to do-
A price so vast as is unknown,
Yet, by His gift, is made thine own.
There's wealth enough; I need no more.
Farewell, my **pelf**; farewell, my store;
The world no longer let me love.
My hope and treasure lie above.

WRITE

NARRATIVE: "Verses upon the Burning of Our House" describes the speaker's resilience after losing her home. Write a narrative about a character who also demonstrates resilience during a time of trial, or write a personal narrative describing a similar experience from your own life in order to create a deeper connection to the themes of the text.

The Scarlet Letter

FICTION
Nathaniel Hawthorne
1850

Introduction

The Scarlet Letter is a classic novel by Nathaniel Hawthorne (1804–1864), a towering figure in 19th-century American literature whose dark, allegorical fiction broods on America's deeply Puritanical origins. The protagonist of *The Scarlet Letter* is Hester Prynne, a young mother of a newborn baby living in the Puritan settlement of Boston in 17th-century New England. Branded as an adulteress and sentenced to wear a scarlet "A" as her badge of shame, Hester must endure the judgment of the strict, mean-spirited townspeople. In this excerpt, after defiantly refusing to disclose the identity of the baby's father, Hester is led to the town square for public shaming.

". . . in fine red cloth, surrounded with an elaborate embroidery . . . , appeared the letter A."

NOTES

from Chapter II. THE MARKET-PLACE

The Scarlet Letter by Hugues Merle, 1861

1 The grass-plot before the jail, in Prison Lane, on a certain summer morning, not less than two centuries ago, was occupied by a pretty large number of the inhabitants of Boston, all with their eyes intently fastened on the iron-clamped oaken door. Amongst any other population, or at a later period in the history of New England, the grim rigidity that petrified the bearded physiognomies of these good people would have augured some awful business in hand. It could have betokened nothing short of the anticipated execution of some noted culprit, on whom the sentence of a legal tribunal had but confirmed the verdict of public sentiment. But, in that early severity of the Puritan[1] character, an inference of this kind could not so indubitably be drawn. It might be that a sluggish bond-servant, or an undutiful child, whom his parents had given over to the civil authority, was to be corrected at the whipping-post. It might be that an Antinomian, a Quaker, or other heterodox religionist, was to be scourged out of the town, or an idle or vagrant Indian, whom the white man's firewater had made riotous about the streets, was to be driven with stripes into the shadow of the forest. It might be, too, that a witch, like old Mistress Hibbins, the bitter-tempered widow of the magistrate, was to die upon the gallows. In either case, there was very much the same solemnity of demeanour on the part of the spectators, as befitted a people among whom religion and law were almost identical, and in whose character both were so thoroughly interfused, that the mildest and severest acts of public **discipline** were alike made venerable and awful. . .

2 "Goodwives," said a hard-featured dame of fifty, "I'll tell ye a piece of my mind. It would be greatly for the public behoof if we women, being of mature age

1. **Puritan** a Protestant religious group in New England marked by their rigid moral code

NOTES

and church-members in good repute, should have the handling of such malefactresses as this Hester Prynne. What think ye, gossips? If the hussy stood up for judgment before us five, that are now here in a knot together, would she come off with such a sentence as the worshipful **magistrates** have awarded? Marry, I trow not."

3 "People say," said another, "that the Reverend Master Dimmesdale, her godly pastor, takes it very grievously to heart that such a scandal should have come upon his congregation."

4 "The magistrates are God-fearing gentlemen, but merciful overmuch—that is a truth," added a third autumnal matron. "At the very least, they should have put the brand of a hot iron on Hester Prynne's forehead. Madame Hester would have winced at that, I warrant me. But she—the naughty baggage—little will she care what they put upon the bodice of her gown! Why, look you, she may cover it with a brooch, or such like heathenish adornment, and so walk the streets as brave as ever!"

5 "Ah, but," interposed, more softly, a young wife, holding a child by the hand, "let her cover the mark as she will, the pang of it will be always in her heart."

6 "What do we talk of marks and brands, whether on the bodice of her gown or the flesh of her forehead?" cried another female, the ugliest as well as the most pitiless of these self-constituted judges. "This woman has brought shame upon us all, and ought to die; is there not law for it? Truly there is, both in the Scripture and the statute-book. Then let the magistrates, who have made it of no effect, thank themselves if their own wives and daughters go astray."

7 "Mercy on us, goodwife!" exclaimed a man in the crowd, "is there no virtue in woman, save what springs from a wholesome fear of the gallows? That is the hardest word yet! Hush now, gossips; for the lock is turning in the prison-door, and here comes Mistress Prynne herself."

8 The door of the jail being flung open from within there appeared, in the first place, like a black shadow emerging into sunshine, the grim and gristly presence of the town-beadle, with a sword by his side, and his staff of office in his hand. This personage prefigured and represented in his aspect the whole **dismal** severity of the Puritanic code of law, which it was his business to administer in its final and closest application to the offender. Stretching forth the official staff in his left hand, he laid his right upon the shoulder of a young woman, whom he thus drew forward, until, on the threshold of the prison-door, she repelled him, by an action marked with natural dignity and force of character, and stepped into the open air as if by her own free will. She bore in her arms a child, a baby of some three months old, who winked and turned aside its little face from the too **vivid** light of day; because its

NOTES

existence, heretofore, had brought it acquaintance only with the grey twilight of a dungeon, or other darksome apartment of the prison.

9 When the young woman—the mother of this child—stood fully revealed before the crowd, it seemed to be her first impulse to clasp the infant closely to her bosom; not so much by an impulse of motherly affection, as that she might thereby conceal a certain token, which was wrought or fastened into her dress. In a moment, however, wisely judging that one token of her shame would but poorly serve to hide another, she took the baby on her arm, and with a burning blush, and yet a haughty smile, and a glance that would not be abashed, looked around at her townspeople and neighbours. On the breast of her gown, in fine red cloth, surrounded with an **elaborate** embroidery and fantastic flourishes of gold thread, appeared the letter A. It was so artistically done, and with so much fertility and gorgeous luxuriance of fancy, that it had all the effect of a last and fitting decoration to the apparel which she wore, and which was of a splendour in accordance with the taste of the age, but greatly beyond what was allowed by the sumptuary regulations of the colony.

WRITE

LITERARY ANALYSIS: *The Scarlet Letter* depicts life in a society where Puritan values are the norm. What details about the historical and social setting of this society contribute to the plot and how people in the crowd perceive Hester? Use evidence from the text to support your response.

I, Tituba, Black Witch of Salem

FICTION
Maryse Condé
1986

Introduction

Maryse Condé (b. 1937) is a French-language author from Guadeloupe best known for writing historical fiction, most notably *Segu* (1987) and *I, Tituba, Black Witch of Salem* (1986). Condé's politically-charged works center on African and Caribbean culture, specifically the Caribbean diaspora, and themes of racism, feminism, and colonialism. *I, Tituba, Black Witch of Salem* is the fictionalized story of Tituba, a real Barbadian woman who was tried as a witch during the Salem witch trials. Tituba had been represented as a fictionalized character prior to Condé's work in Arthur Miller's 1953 play, *The Crucible*. In this excerpt, Condé takes us into the world of Tituba as she entertains the young girls of Salem.

"'Tituba can do anything. Tituba knows everything. Tituba sees everything.'"

NOTES

1 I now had my kitchen full of little girls. I didn't like them all. I took a special dislike to Anne Putnam[1], and the little servant girl, Mercy Lewis, who was about the same age and **accompanied** her everywhere. There was something in those two girls that made me have doubts about the innocence of childhood. Perhaps children cannot escape the frustrations and lasciviousness of adults after all. Whatever the case, Anne and Mercy reminded me constantly of Samuel Parris's speeches on Satan's presence in all of us. The same was true for Abigail. I sensed a violent streak in her, the power of her imagination to give a particular twist to the slightest everyday incident and this hatred—no, the word is not too strong—this hatred she had for the adult world, as if she could not forgive it for building a coffin around her youth.

2 Although I didn't like them all, I pitied them with their waxen skin and their bodies so full of promise yet mutilated like those trees that gardeners try to dwarf. In contrast, our childhood as little slaves, bitter though it was, seemed glowing, lit up by the joy of our games, our rambles, and our rovings together. We floated rafts made of sugarcane on the rushing streams. We grilled pink and yellow fish on little crisscrosses of green wood. We danced. And it was this pity of mine, against which I was helpless, that made me tolerate these children around me and encouraged me to entertain them. I wouldn't stop until I had managed to get one of them to burst out laughing and plead: "Tituba! Oh, Tituba!"

3 Their favorite stories were about people in league with the devil. They sat in a circle around me and I could smell the sharp scent of their sparingly washed bodies. They assailed me with questions.

4 "Tituba, do you think there are people in league with the devil living in Salem?"

---

1. **Anne Putnam** Many of the novel's characters are also depicted in Arthur Miller's *The Crucible*—including Samuel Parris, Abigail Williams, Elizabeth Proctor, and Putnam, one of the primary accusers of the Salem witch trials, and an important, critical witness during the trial proceedings.

NOTES

5 I nodded and laughed. "Yes, I think Sarah Good must be one." Sarah Good was still a young woman, but she was hunched over and a beggar. The children were afraid of her because of the stinking pipe she always had stuck between her teeth and because of her constant muttering. It seemed as if she was mumbling prayers that nobody could understand except herself. Apart from that, she was a generous soul, at least I thought so.

6 "Do you think so, Tituba?" the children cheeped. "And Sarah Osborne, is she one too?"

7 Sarah Osborne was an old woman, not a beggar like the other Sarah, but well-off, the owner of a lovely oak-paneled house, who in her youth had **committed** some fault or other to her discredit.

8 I took a deep breath and pretended to think hard, letting them stew in their curiosity, before **solemnly** declaring: "Perhaps!"

9 Abigail insisted. "Have you seen them both fly with their skin all scorched? And Elizabeth Proctor, have you seen her? Have you?"

10 Mistress Proctor was one of the nicest women in the village, the only one who was kind enough to talk to me about slavery, about the country I came from and its inhabitants.

11 "You know very well, Abigail, that I'm joking," I said severely. And I sent everyone away.

12 When I was left alone with Betsey she, too, asked me in her high-pitched voice: "Do people in league with the devil actually exist, Tituba? Do they?"

13 I took her in my arms. "What does it matter? Aren't I here to protect you if they try to harm you?"

14 She looked straight at me and a shadow that I tried to **dispel** was dancing in the back of her eyes.

15 "Tituba knows the words that cure every sickness, that heal every wound, and untie every knot. Don't you know that?"

16 She remained silent, her body trembling even more **despite** my words of consolation. I hugged her up against me and the wings of her heart beat desperately like a bird in a cage, while I said over and over again: "Tituba can do anything. Tituba knows everything. Tituba sees everything."

Excerpted from *I, Tituba, Black Witch of Salem* by Maryse Condé, published by the University of Virginia Press.

WRITE

ARGUMENTATIVE: In *I, Tituba, Black Witch of Salem*, Tituba befriends a group of young, Puritan girls. Who has power in this text? Tituba? The girls? Someone else? Determine who has power in the text, and argue your position using evidence from the text. As you support your position, be sure to explain what it means to have power.

The Crucible

DRAMA
Arthur Miller
1953

Introduction

Arthur Miller (1915–2005) was a prolific American playwright. In 1956, he was tried before the House Un-American Activities Committee based on his personal affiliations and the nature of his work. Modeled after the Salem witchcraft trials of 1692, Arthur Miller's *The Crucible* is an allegory of the anti-Communist "witch-hunts" of the 1950s carried out by Senator Joseph McCarthy and the House Un-American Activities Committee. In this opening scene, Samuel Parris's daughter Betty is unconscious after a night of dancing in the woods with several girls and the family servant, Tituba. The townspeople blame her illness on witchcraft.

"There is a murdering witch among us, bound to keep herself in the dark."

NOTES

Skill: Dramatic Elements and Structure

The stage directions tell me where and when the play is set. The lack of furniture and the comment about "spareness" give an air of severity and suggest the characters will also have these qualities.

from Act I (An Overture)

1 *A small upper bedroom in the home of Reverend Samuel Parris, Salem, Massachusetts, in the spring of the year 1692.*

2 There is a narrow window at the left. Through its leaded panes the morning sunlight streams. A candle still burns near the bed, which is at the right. A chest, a chair, and a small table are the other furnishings. At the back a door opens on the landing of the stairway to the ground floor. The room gives off an air of clean spareness. The roof rafters are **exposed,** and the wood colors are raw and unmellowed.

3 As the curtain rises, Reverend Parris is discovered kneeling beside the bed, evidently in prayer. His daughter, Betty Parris, aged ten, is lying on the bed, inert.

. . .

4 [H]is niece, Abigail Williams, seventeen, enters—a strikingly beautiful girl, an orphan, with an endless capacity for dissembling. Now she is all worry and apprehension and **propriety.**

5 ABIGAIL: Uncle? *He looks to her.* Susanna Walcott's here from Doctor Griggs.

6 PARRIS: Oh? Let her come, let her come.

7 ABIGAIL, *leaning out the door to call to Susanna, who is down the hall a few steps:* Come in, Susanna.

8 *Susanna Walcott, a little younger than Abigail, a nervous, hurried girl, enters.*

9 PARRIS, *eagerly:* What does the doctor say, child?

10 SUSANNA, *craning around Parris to get a look at Betty.* He bid me come and tell you, reverend sir, that he cannot discover no medicine for it in his books.

11 PARRIS: Then he must search on.

12 SUSANNA: Aye, sir, he have been searchin' his books since he left you, sir. But he bid me tell you, that you might look to unnatural things for the cause of it.

13 PARRIS, *his eyes going wide:* No—no. There be no unnatural cause here. Tell him I have sent for Reverend Hale of Beverly, and Mr. Hale will surely confirm that. Let him look to medicine and put out all thought of unnatural causes here. There be none.

14 SUSANNA: Aye, sir. He bid me tell you. *She turns to go.*

15 ABIGAIL: Speak nothin' of it in the village, Susanna.

16 PARRIS: Go directly home and speak nothing of unnatural causes.

17 SUSANNA: Aye, sir. I pray for her. *She goes out.*

18 ABIGAIL: Uncle, the rumor of witchcraft is all about; I think you'd best go down and deny it yourself. The parlor's packed with people, sir. I'll sit with her.

19 PARRIS, *pressed, turns on her:* And what shall I say to them? That my daughter and my niece I discovered dancing like heathen in the forest?

20 ABIGAIL: Uncle, we did dance; let you tell them I confessed it—and I'll be whipped if I must be. But they're speaking of witchcraft. Betty's not witched.

21 PARRIS: Abigail, I cannot go before the congregation when I know you have not opened with me. What did you do with her in the forest?

22 ABIGAIL: We did dance, uncle, and when you leaped out of the bush so suddenly, Betty was frightened and then she fainted. And there's the whole of it.

23 PARRIS: Child. Sit you down.

24 ABIGAIL, *quivering, as she sits:* I would never hurt Betty. I love her dearly.

25 PARRIS: Now look you, child, your punishment will come in its time. But if you **trafficked** with spirits in the forest I must know it now, for surely my enemies will, and they will ruin me with it.

26 ABIGAIL: But we never conjured spirits.

NOTES

Skill: Textual Evidence

As rational explanations are taken away, Parris's panic grows because of the uncertainty about Betty's condition.

NOTES

Skill: Textual Evidence

I can tell that Parris is panicked from his questioning. We still don't know what happened to Betty. Also, the audience is learning about the conflict in the town. All of this means the mood onstage is really tense.

27 PARRIS: Then why can she not move herself since midnight? This child is desperate! *Abigail lowers her eyes.* It must come out—my enemies will bring it out. Let me know what you done there. Abigail, do you understand that I have many enemies?

28 ABIGAIL: I have heard of it, uncle.

29 PARRIS: There is a faction that is sworn to drive me from my pulpit. Do you understand that?

30 ABIGAIL: I think so, sir.

31 PARRIS: Now then, in the midst of such disruption, my own household is discovered to be the very center of some obscene practice. Abominations are done in the forest—

32 ABIGAIL: It were sport, uncle!

33 PARRIS, *pointing at Betty:* You call this sport? *She lowers her eyes. He pleads:* Abigail, if you know something that may help the doctor, for God's sake tell it to me. *She is silent.* I saw Tituba waving her arms over the fire when I came on you. Why was she doing that? And I heard a screeching and gibberish coming from her mouth. She were swaying like a dumb beast over that fire!

34 ABIGAIL: She always sings her Barbados[1] songs, and we dance.

35 PARRIS: I cannot blink what I saw, Abigail, for my enemies will not blink it. I saw a dress lying on the grass.

36 ABIGAIL, *innocently:* A dress?

37 PARRIS—*it is very hard to say:* Aye, a dress. And I thought I saw—someone naked running through the trees!

38 ABIGAIL, *in terror:* No one was naked! You mistake yourself, uncle!

39 PARRIS, *with anger:* I saw it! *He moves from her. Then, resolved:* Now tell me true, Abigail. And I pray you feel the weight of truth upon you, for now my ministry's at stake, my ministry and perhaps your cousin's life. Whatever abomination you have done, give me all of it now, for I dare not be taken unaware when I go before them down there.

40 ABIGAIL: There is nothin' more. I swear it, uncle.

1. **Barbados** a Caribbean island settled by the Spanish, who would use the island to bring enslaved people to the Americas

NOTES

41 PARRIS, *studies her, then nods, half convinced:* Abigail, I have fought here three long years to bend these stiff-necked people to me, and now, just now when some good respect is rising for me in the parish, you compromise my very character. I have given you a home, child, I have put clothes upon your back—now give me upright answer. Your name in the town—it is entirely white, is it not?

42 ABIGAIL, *with an edge of resentment:* Why, I am sure it is, sir. There be no blush about my name.

43 PARRIS, *to the point:* Abigail, is there any other cause than you have told me, for your being discharged from Goody Proctor's service? I have heard it said, and I tell you as I heard it, that she comes so rarely to the church this year for she will not sit so close to something soiled. What signified that remark?

44 ABIGAIL: She hates me, uncle, she must, for I would not be her slave. It's a bitter woman, a lying, cold, sniveling woman, and I will not work for such a woman!

45 PARRIS: She may be. And yet it has troubled me that you are now seven month out of their house, and in all this time no other family has ever called for your service.

46 ABIGAIL: They want slaves, not such as I. Let them send to Barbados for that. I will not black my face for any of them! *With ill-concealed resentment at him:* Do you begrudge my bed, uncle?

47 PARRIS: No—no.

48 ABIGAIL, *in a temper:* My name is good in the village! I will not have it said my name is soiled! Goody Proctor is a gossiping liar!

49 *Enter Mrs. Ann Putnam. She is a twisted soul of forty-five, a death-ridden woman, haunted by dreams.*

50 PARRIS, *as soon as the door begins to open:* No—no, I cannot have anyone. *He sees her, and a certain deference springs into him, although his worry remains.* Why, Goody Putnam, come in.

51 MRS. PUTNAM. *full of breath, shiny-eyed:* It is a marvel. It is surely a stroke of hell upon you.

52 PARRIS: No, Goody Putnam, it is—

53 MRS. PUTNAM, *glancing at Betty:* How high did she fly, how high?

54 PARRIS: No, no, she never flew—

NOTES

55 MRS. PUTNAM, *very pleased with it:* Why, it's sure she did. Mr. Collins saw her goin' over Ingersoll's barn, and come down light as bird, he says!

56 PARRIS: Now, look you, Goody Putnam, she never—*Enter Thomas Putnam, a well-to-do, hard-handed landowner, near fifty.* Oh, good morning, Mr. Putnam.

57 PUTNAM: It is a providence the thing is out now! It is a providence. *He goes directly to the bed.*

58 PARRIS: What's out, sir, what's—?

59 *Mrs. Putnam goes to the bed.*

60 PUTNAM, *looking down at Betty:* Why, *her* eyes is closed! Look you, Ann.

61 MRS. PUTNAM: Why, that's strange. *To Parris:* Ours is open.

62 PARRIS, *shocked:* Your Ruth is sick?

63 MRS. PUTNAM, *with vicious certainty:* I'd not call it sick; the Devil's touch is heavier than sick. Its death, y'know, it's death drivin' into them, forked and hoofed.

64 PARRIS: Oh, pray not! Why, how does Ruth ail?

65 MRS. PUTNAM: She ails as she must—she never waked this morning, but her eyes open and she walks, and hears naught, sees naught, and cannot eat. Her soul is taken, surely.

66 *Parris is struck.*

67 PUTNAM, *as though for further details:* They say you've sent for Reverend Hale of Beverly?

68 PARRIS, *with dwindling conviction now:* A precaution only. He has much experience in all demonic arts, and I—

69 MRS. PUTNAM: He has indeed; and found a witch in Beverly last year, and let you remember that.

70 PARRIS: Now, Goody Ann, they only thought that were a witch, and I am certain there be no element of witchcraft here.

71 PUTNAM: No witchcraft! Now look you, Mr. Parris—

72 PARRIS: Thomas, Thomas, I pray you, leap not to witchcraft. I know that you—you least of all, Thomas, would ever wish so disastrous a charge laid upon me. We cannot leap to witchcraft. They will howl me out of Salem for such corruption in my house.

73 A word about Thomas Putnam. He was a man with many grievances, at least one of which appears justified. Some time before, his wife's brother-in-law, James Bayley, had been turned down as minister of Salem. Bayley had all the qualifications, and a two-thirds vote into the bargain, but a faction stopped his acceptance, for reasons that are not clear.

74 Thomas Putnam was the eldest son of the richest man in the village. He had fought the Indians at Narragansett[2], and was deeply interested in parish affairs. He undoubtedly felt it poor payment that the village should so blatantly disregard his candidate for one of its more important offices, especially since he regarded himself as the intellectual superior of most of the people around him.

75 His vindictive nature was demonstrated long before the witchcraft began. A former Salem minister, George Burroughs, had had to borrow money to pay for his wife's funeral, and, since the parish was **remiss** in his salary, he was soon bankrupt. Thomas and his brother John had Burroughs jailed for debts the man did not owe. The incident is important only in that Burroughs succeeded in becoming minister where Bayley, Thomas Putnam's brother-in-law, had been rejected; the motif of resentment is clear here. Thomas Putnam felt that his own name and the honor of his family had been smirched by the village, and he meant to right matters however he could.

76 Another reason to believe him a deeply embittered man was his attempt to break his father's will, which left a disproportionate amount to a stepbrother. As with every other public cause in which he tried to force his way, he failed in this.

77 So it is not surprising to find that so many accusations against people are in the handwriting of Thomas Putnam, or that his name is so often found as a witness corroborating the supernatural testimony, or that his daughter led the crying-out at the most opportune junctures of the trials, especially when—But we'll speak of that when we come to it.

78 PUTNAM—*at the moment he is intent upon getting Parris, for whom he has only contempt, to move toward the abyss:* Mr. Parris, I have taken your part in all contention here, and I would continue; but I cannot if you hold back in this. There are hurtful, vengeful spirits layin' hands on these children.

2. **Indians at Narragansett** a Native American tribe living in what is now known as Narragansett, Rhode Island

NOTES

Skill: Dramatic Elements and Structure

The italics reveals that Mr. Putnam has "only contempt" for Parris, which is different than what he says to Parris. This dramatic tension previews plot events to come and hints that people will turn against each other.

NOTES

79 PARRIS: But, Thomas, you cannot—

80 PUTNAM: Ann! Tell Mr. Parris what you have done.

81 MRS. PUTNAM: Reverend Parris, I have laid seven babies unbaptized in the earth. Believe me, sir, you never saw more hearty babies born. And yet, each would wither in my arms the very night of their birth. I have spoke nothin', but my heart has clamored intimations. And now, this year, my Ruth, my only—I see her turning strange. A secret child she has become this year, and shrivels like a sucking mouth were pullin' on her life too. And so I thought to send her to your Tituba—

82 PARRIS: To Tituba! What may Tituba—?

83 MRS. PUTNAM: Tituba knows how to speak to the dead, Mr. Parris.

84 PARRIS: Goody Ann, it is a **formidable** sin to conjure up the dead!

85 MRS. PUTNAM: I take it on my soul, but who else may surely tell us what person murdered my babies?

86 PARRIS, *horrified:* Woman!

87 MRS. PUTNAM: They were murdered, Mr. Parris! And mark this proof! Mark it! Last night my Ruth were ever so close to their little spirits; I know it, sir. For how else is she struck dumb now except some power of darkness would stop her mouth? It is a marvelous sign, Mr. Parris!

88 PUTNAM: Don't you understand it, sir? There is a murdering witch among us, bound to keep herself in the dark. *Parris turns to Betty, a frantic terror rising in him.* Let your enemies make of it what they will, you cannot blink it more.

89 PARRIS, *to Abigail:* Then you were conjuring spirits last night.

90 ABIGAIL, *whispering:* Not I, sir—Tituba and Ruth.

91 PARRIS *turns now, with new fear, and goes to Betty, looks down at her, and then, gazing off:* Oh, Abigail, what proper payment for my charity! Now I am undone.

First Read

Read *The Crucible*. After you read, complete the Think Questions below.

THINK QUESTIONS

1. What role does Parris play in the community? Use details from the text to explain how this might influence the future action of the story.

2. What is Parris trying to learn from Abigail? Why is he so intent on getting a truthful response? Cite evidence from the text to support your answer.

3. What do you learn about Ann Putnam's beliefs regarding witchcraft in this excerpt? Cite evidence from the text to support your answer.

4. What is the meaning of the word **trafficked** as it is used in the text? Write your best definition here, along with a brief explanation of how you arrived at its meaning.

5. The Latin word *remissus* means "slackened." With this information in mind and using context clues from the text, write your best definition of the word **remiss** here.

Skill: Dramatic Elements and Structure

Use the Checklist to analyze Dramatic Elements and Structure in *The Crucible*. Refer to the sample student annotations about Dramatic Elements and Structure in the text.

••• CHECKLIST FOR DRAMATIC ELEMENTS AND STRUCTURE

In order to determine the author's choices regarding the development of a drama, note the following:

- ✓ the names of all the characters, how they are introduced, and their relationships with one another
- ✓ character development, including personality traits, motivations, decisions they make, and actions they take
- ✓ the setting(s) of the story and how it influences the characters and the events of the plot
- ✓ how character choices and dialogue affect the plot
- ✓ the stage directions and how they are used to reveal character and plot development

To analyze the impact of the author's choices regarding how to develop and relate elements of a story or drama, consider the following questions:

- ✓ How does the order of events in the play affect the development of the drama?
- ✓ How are characters introduced, and what does it reveal about them?
- ✓ In what ways do the characters change over the course of the drama?
- ✓ How do the choices the characters make help advance the plot?
- ✓ How does the setting affect the characters and plot?
- ✓ How do the characters' actions help develop the theme or message of the play?

Skill: Dramatic Elements and Structure

Reread paragraphs 49–55 of *The Crucible*. Then, using the Checklist on the previous page, answer the multiple-choice questions below.

YOUR TURN

1. How does Samuel Parris's mood change during his conversation with Mrs. Ann Putnam?

   ○ A. He feels relieved that Ann agrees with his opinions.
   ○ B. He is welcoming and courteous to Ann.
   ○ C. He is happy to have Ann provide more details about what happened.
   ○ D. He becomes increasingly frustrated by Ann's claims.

2. How does the introduction of Mrs. Putnam and her response to Betty lying on the bed help the reader understand Mrs. Putnam?

   ○ A. Mrs. Putnam should be trusted as a character because of her belief in supernatural events.
   ○ B. Mrs. Putnam accepts supernatural explanations because of the pain she is in.
   ○ C. Mrs. Putnam is angry at Betty, which suggests that she has a lot of pain.
   ○ D. Mrs. Putnam's explanation of events is correct, which means that Reverend Parris is lying.

Skill: Textual Evidence

Use the Checklist to analyze Textual Evidence in *The Crucible*. Refer to the sample student annotations about Textual Evidence in the text.

••• CHECKLIST FOR TEXTUAL EVIDENCE

In order to support an analysis by citing evidence that is explicitly stated in the text, do the following:

- ✓ read the text closely and critically
- ✓ identify what the text says explicitly
- ✓ find the most relevant textual evidence that supports your analysis
- ✓ consider why an author explicitly states specific details and information
- ✓ cite the specific words, phrases, sentences, or paragraphs from the text that support your analysis
- ✓ determine where evidence in the text still leaves certain matters uncertain or unresolved

In order to interpret implicit meanings in a text by making inferences, do the following:

- ✓ Combine information directly stated in the text with your own knowledge, experiences, and observations.
- ✓ Cite the specific words, phrases, sentences, or paragraphs from the text that led to and support this inference.

In order to cite textual evidence to support an analysis of what the text says explicitly as well as inferences drawn from the text, consider the following questions:

- ✓ Have I read the text closely and critically?
- ✓ What inferences am I making about the text?
- ✓ What textual evidence am I using to support these inferences?
- ✓ Am I quoting the evidence from the text correctly?
- ✓ Does my textual evidence logically relate to my analysis or the inference I am making?
- ✓ Does evidence in the text still leave certain matters unanswered or unresolved? In what ways?

Skill: Textual Evidence

Reread paragraphs 40–47 of *The Crucible*. Then, using the Checklist on the previous page, answer the multiple-choice questions below.

YOUR TURN

1. This question has two parts. First, answer Part A. Then, answer Part B.

Part A: Which of the following questions best states an uncertainty that remains at the end of this exchange between Parris and Abigail?

- ○ A. Why does Parris distrust Abigail?
- ○ B. Why does Goody Proctor dislike Abigail?
- ○ C. Why would Goody Proctor lie about Abigail?
- ○ D. Why does Abigail dislike Goody Proctor?

Part B: Which line of dialogue from the passage best supports your answer from Part A?

- ○ A. "PARRIS, *studies her, then nods, half convinced:* Abigail, I have fought here three long years to bend these stiff-necked people to me, and now, just now when some good respect is rising for me in the parish, you compromise my very character."
- ○ B. "ABIGAIL: She hates me, uncle, she must, for I would not be her slave. It's a bitter woman, a lying, cold, sniveling woman, and I will not work for such a woman!"
- ○ C. "PARRIS: She may be. And yet it has troubled me that you are now seven month out of their house, and in all this time no other family has ever called for your service."
- ○ D. "ABIGAIL: They want slaves, not such as I. Let them send to Barbados for that. I will not black my face for any of them!"

Close Read

Reread *The Crucible*. As you reread, complete the Skills Focus questions below. Then use your answers and annotations from the questions to help you complete the Write activity.

SKILLS FOCUS

1. Identify details about the two settings in the text and explain what they represent in terms of religious beliefs.
2. Explain how Parris's and Abigail's differing descriptions of what happened in the woods the previous night affect the atmosphere of the scene.
3. Identify evidence which demonstrates why Arthur Miller may have represented Parris and Abigail's discussion about what happened in the forest the previous night rather than beginning the play with the girls in the woods. Explain how the evidence from the text you've chosen addresses your reasoning.
4. Identify evidence that either Parris is being paranoid or he has good reason to fear that his reputation will be ruined and he will be driven from his pulpit.
5. Describe how the characters in this scene from *The Crucible* are independent from or dependent on each other.

WRITE

LITERARY ANALYSIS: In *The Scarlet Letter; I Tituba, Black Witch of Salem*; and *The Crucible*, the authors represent characters who are in some way outside of their societies. In a written response, analyze the ways in which these representations reflect or challenge the notion that independence defines the American spirit. Support your response with evidence from the text.

LITERARY SEMINAR:

Revolutionary Thinking

Introduction

The citizens of Britain's American colonies found themselves at the forefront of political transformation at the end of the French and Indian Wars. Discontented and developing a personality separate from that of their "home" country, Americans were inspired by new ideas about human liberty fed by philosophers of the Enlightenment such as John Locke. The moment would produce nothing less than a country founded on ideals that would eventually undo the rule of kings.

". . . huge moral, intellectual, and religious shifts blew through Europe and America and upended the status quo."

NOTES

1 Leading up to the Revolutionary War[1], America was transitioning from a colonial identity to a national one. The French and Indian War[2] had recently ended, and although the British military won, the enormous expenses pushed onto the colonies helped to sow the seeds of rebellion. Additionally, huge moral, intellectual, and religious shifts blew through Europe and America and upended the status quo. A boom in literacy and wide publication of political writing led to conversations about American philosophy, morality, and ideas happening in the public sphere in a very significant way.

The Enlightenment's Influence on American Philosophy & Governance

Cartoon entitled "Join, Or Die." The first known American cartoon. Published by Benjamin Franklin in 1754, supporting his plan for a colonial union. Presented at the Albany Congress.

2 The European intellectual movement known as the Enlightenment crossed over into America during the eighteenth century by way of many thought leaders of the time, including Benjamin Franklin and Thomas Jefferson, and their writing. The key **aspect** of this movement was the belief that people could use reason to understand the universe and make the world a better place, which in turn had a dramatic effect on the place of religion in society. The movement was fueled by advances in science and mathematics that

1. **Revolutionary War** the war between the American colonies and Great Britain that resulted in the colonies' independence
2. **French and Indian War** a war lasting from 1754 to 1763 in which France and Britain fought over territory in the present day United States, each side aided by different groups of Native American allies

NOTES

created a model of the world and universe different from that of traditional religious teachings. Enlightenment thinkers tended to be Deists, meaning that their moral focus did not depend on scripture, specifically.

3 One of America's most famous intellectuals, Benjamin Franklin, was also a thinker of the Enlightenment. In addition to much of his scientific work that rejected traditional explanations for natural events, such as lightning, Franklin was also a moral thinker. His letter, "The Whistle," is an example of a developing American morality, philosophical as well as useful, and not necessarily stemming from religion.

4 Perhaps the Enlightenment thinker to have the most dramatic effect on American thinking and writing was John Locke. Locke was one of England's most significant **theorists** in the areas of philosophy and political science. In 1690 Locke wrote his major work in political philosophy, the *Two Treatises of Government*. The first of these treatises was an argument against the concept of the divine right of monarchs and the British patriarchy. It is the *Second Treatise on Government,* though, that has come to be seen as Locke's masterpiece.

5 In his second treatise, Locke argues that the basic condition of the human race is a state of nature in which people are entirely free. Locke believed that human beings are endowed by God with reason, so they should be allowed to make laws to govern themselves. He also noted, however, that some people have a tendency toward injustice and violence, so people need to enter into a compact with one another to form a government to protect themselves from crimes. If the government denies people their liberty or their property, they may rebel and replace their leaders.

6 Echoes of Locke can be found in the Declaration of Independence, whose primary author was Thomas Jefferson. In the second paragraph of the Declaration, Jefferson writes that people "are endowed by their Creator with certain unalienable rights, that among these are Life, Liberty and the pursuit of Happiness." Locke identifies basic rights as "life, liberty and property," so Jefferson expands the definition **somewhat**.

7 Thomas Paine was inspired by fundamental Enlightenment ideals in his 1776 pamphlet *Common Sense*, which had a dramatic effect on support for the war. Benjamin Franklin observed that he had not heard any American speaking in favor of independence before the publication of *Common Sense*. After publication of the pamphlet, many areas of the colonies favored separating from the British government.

8 In *Common Sense,* Paine references "natural rights," similar to Locke's description of the rights people possess as the result of natural law. However, in contrast to Locke, Paine is more negative about the role of government. In Paine's pamphlet, government "in its best state is but a necessary evil," and the least amount of government gives the greatest amount of liberty. Later, his pamphlets entitled *The Crisis* and published from 1776 through 1783 were

NOTES

read aloud at military campgrounds, and bolstered the argument for the need to rebel against England.

9 Throughout this period, Revolutionaries were bandying about questions of power and independence, and these ideas are reflected in Abigail Adams's "Letters to John Adams." In one, dated March 31, 1776, Adams implores her husband to "remember the ladies" in a famous call to bear gender equality in mind at the formation of a new government.

10 When the framers of the Constitution sat down to determine the methods of governance they would use, they had a great deal of influence. Clearly, they were rebelling against the style of governance present in England, seeking out a more representative and democratic style of government. Additionally, there is evidence that the Framers looked to the group of tribes known as the Iroquois, for the federal relationship between a central government and the individual tribes.

A Question of National Identity

11 In another letter from Abigail Adams to her husband, John Adams, we see her directly naming the hypocrisy of slavery in the midst of a fight for independence. While the nation was grappling with what it meant to rebel against its mother country, an irony was also brewing in conversations about freedom and independence: slavery. While many Quakers (members of a religious group) had been campaigning against slavery since the 17th century, the majority of colonists did not seriously question the issue until later in the 19th century. Olaudah Equiano's *The Interesting Narrative of the Life of Olaudah Equiano, or Gustavus Vassa, the African* demonstrates the pain and suffering the slave trade caused on an individual level. It also reflects the larger conversation about abolition and ending the slave trade that was happening not just in America, but in England as well.

12 While a political and philosophical movement was taking place in America, a religious revival called the Great Awakening was changing the relationship many Christians had with God to be more personal. On that note, slave owners were encouraged to provide a basic education to enslaved peoples, so that they could independently read the Bible and be **converted** to Christianity. The work of poets like Phillis Wheatley and Jupiter Hammon are evidence of this trend. For instance, Phillis Wheatley's poem "On Being Brought from Africa to America" explores race, equality, and religion, and reflects the complexities of the developing American identity and the **ongoing** hypocrisies inherent in a nation championing independence that continued to enslave people.

13 The ideals set forth by Thomas Jefferson and Thomas Paine remain central to the idea of what it means to be a citizen in the United States. The religious and moral conversations had during the revolution helped develop a uniquely American ethos. By looking to these and other publications, we can better understand the ideas that were circulated and debated to form the country we live in today.

Literary Seminar: Revolutionary Thinking

Read "Literary Seminar: Revolutionary Thinking." After you read, complete the Think Questions below.

THINK QUESTIONS

1. Why were the colonists feeling rebellious after the French and Indian War? What change were they looking to make? Explain using evidence from the text to support your ideas.

2. What was new about the writings of John Locke? How old were his Treatises at the time of the American Revolution? Explain using evidence from the text to support your response.

3. According to Abigail Adams (and others), what was the great hypocrisy in the midst of the movement for American independence? Explain with evidence from the text.

4. What is the meaning of the word **somewhat** as it is used in the text? What part of speech is it? Write your best definition of *somewhat* and explain how you figured it out. Check your answer with a dictionary.

5. What is the meaning of the word **convert** as it is used in the text? Write your best definition of *convert* and explain how you figured it out. Verify your answer with a dictionary.

On Being Brought from Africa to America

POETRY
Phillis Wheatley
1773

Introduction

Seized from her home in West Africa by slave traders when she was no more than seven years of age, Phillis Wheatley (ca. 1753–1784) nevertheless learned to read and write in a hostile, unfamiliar land. Named for the ship (*Phyllis*) that brought her to America in chains, she would become the first African American writer to have a book of poetry published. Due to prejudices at the time, Wheatley's authorship of her poems was quickly contested. Seventeen Boston men (including John Hancock) signed a preface to Wheatley's volume, verifying her authorship. Wheatley's poems are stylistically complex and sophisticated, with themes focusing on faith, perseverance, and morality. This poem, "On Being Brought from Africa to America," is an autobiographical reflection of Wheatley's journey to America.

"Some view our sable race with scornful eye . . ."

NOTES

'Twas mercy brought me from my ***Pagan*** land,
Taught my **benighted** soul to understand
That there's a God, that there's a *Saviour* too:
Once I redemption neither sought nor knew.
Some view our **sable** race with **scornful** eye,
"Their colour is a **diabolic** die."
Remember, *Christians*, *Negros*[1], black as *Cain*[2],
May be refin'd, and join th' angelic train.

Phil is Wheatley

WRITE

PERSONAL RESPONSE: Consider the emotions and events described in the poem. In your opinion, what would be an appropriate alternate title to convey the speaker's perspective and experiences? Why? Use evidence from the text to support your response.

1. **Negros** common parlance at the time for peoples of African descent
2. **Cain** In the book of Genesis, Cain, the son of Adam, kills his brother, Abel.

An Address to Miss Phillis Wheatley

POEM
Jupiter Hammon
1778

Introduction

Jupiter Hammon (1711–ca. 1806) was America's first published African American poet. His first poem appeared in a broadside in 1761; his second, featured here, was not published until 17 years later. Hammon was born into slavery; although supportive of the abolitionist movement, he was never himself emancipated. A devout Christian, he encouraged enslaved people to look to heaven for salvation from the evils of slavery on Earth. "An Address to Miss Phillis Wheatley" was a direct entreaty to America's first published African American female poet, herself an emancipated Christian. In the poem, Hammon encourages Wheatley to improve as a Christian and become more devout. In the original publication, each stanza was accompanied by a corresponding Bible verse.

"Dear Phillis, seek for heaven's joys, Where we do hope to meet."

I

O come you pious youth! adore
The wisdom of thy God,
In bringing thee from distant shore,
To learn His holy word.

II

Thou mightst been left behind
Amidst a dark abode;
God's tender mercy still combin'd
Thou hast the holy word.

III

Fair wisdom's ways are paths of peace,
And they that walk therein,
Shall reap the joys that never **cease**
And Christ shall be their king.

IV

God's tender mercy brought thee here;
Tost o'er the raging main;[1]
In Christian faith thou hast a share,
Worth all the gold of Spain.

V

While thousands tossed by the sea,
And others settled down,
God's tender mercy set thee free,
From dangers that come down.

VI

That thou a pattern still might be,
To youth of Boston town,
The blessed Jesus set thee free,
From every sinful wound.

NOTES

Skill: Compare and Contrast

Like Wheatley's "On Being Brought from Africa to America," Hammon uses religious imagery.

1. **main** (archaic) the ocean

NOTES

Skill: Compare and Contrast

I notice that this poem uses an ABAB rhyme scheme, though the final word in the third line isn't an exact rhyme. Wheatley's scheme was AABB.

VII
The blessed Jesus, who came down,
Unvail'd his sacred face,
To cleanse the soul of every wound,
And give repenting grace.

VIII
That we poor sinners may obtain
The pardon of our sin;
Dear blessed Jesus now constrain
And bring us flocking in.

IX
Come you, Phillis, now aspire,
And seek the living God,
So step by step thou mayst go higher,
Till perfect in the word.

X
While thousands mov'd to distant shore,
And others left behind,
The blessed Jesus still adore,
Implant this in thy mind.

XI
Thou hast left the **heathen** shore;
Thro' mercy of the Lord,
Among the heathen live no more,
Come magnify thy God.

XII
I pray the living God may be,
The shepherd of thy soul;
His tender mercies still are free,
His mysteries to unfold.

XIII
Thou, Phillis, when thou hunger hast,
Or pantest for thy God;
Jesus Christ is thy **relief**,
Thou hast the holy word.

XIV
The bounteous mercies of the Lord
Are hid beyond the sky,

And holy souls that love His word,
Shall taste them when they die.

XV
These bounteous mercies are from God,
The merits of His Son;
The humble soul that loves his word,
He chooses for His own.

XVI
Come, dear Phillis, be advis'd
To drink Samaria's flood,[2]
There's nothing that shall **suffice**
But Christ's redeeming blood.

XVII
While thousands muse with earthly toys;
And range about the street;
Dear Phillis, seek for heaven's joys,
Where we do hope to meet.

XVIII
When God shall send his summons down
And number saints together
Blest angels chant (Triumphant sound)
Come live with me forever.

XIX
The humble soul shall fly to God,
And leave the things of time.
Stand forth as 'twere at the first word,
To taste things more divine.

XX
Behold! the soul shall waft away,
Whene'er we come to die,
And leave its cottage made of clay,
In twinkling of an eye.

XXI
Now glory be to the Most High,
United praises given
By all on earth, **incessantly**,
And all the hosts of heav'n.

NOTES

Skill: Compare and Contrast

Hammmon uses many short stanzas, instead of one longer stanza. The poem seems to be laying out a series of ideas, whereas Wheatley's poem seems to be making one statement.

2. **Samaria's flood** In Biblical times, Samaria was the capital of the northern kingdom of Israel.

First Read

Read "An Address to Miss Phillis Wheatley." After you read, complete the Think Questions below.

THINK QUESTIONS

1. Who are the "pious youth[s]" the poet addresses in stanza 1? Cite evidence from the text to support your answer.

2. When does the poem first mention Phillis Wheatley (outside of the title)? Why do you think her name appears where it does, relative to the beginning of the poem? Cite evidence from the text to support your answer.

3. What is the poet's prevailing attitude toward Phillis Wheatley? Is this attitude straightforward, or conflicted? Cite evidence from the text to support your answer.

4. Read the following dictionary entry:

   relief
   re•lief /rɪ'li:f/ *noun*

   1. financial assistance to a state, organization, or individual
   2. release from anxiety, pain, or stress
   3. a person replacing another on duty
   4. the state of being accentuated by a backdrop

   Which definition most closely matches the meaning of **relief** as it is used in the text? Write the correct definition of *relief* here, and explain how you figured out its meaning.

5. Use context clues to determine the meaning of **suffice** as it is used in the text. Write your definition here, and describe which clues helped you arrive at it.

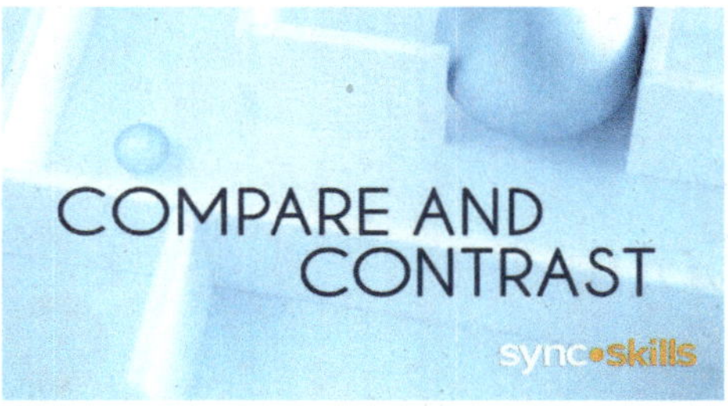

Skill: Compare and Contrast

Use the Checklist to analyze Compare and Contrast in "An Address to Miss Phillis Wheatley" and "On Being Brought from Africa to America."

••• CHECKLIST FOR COMPARE AND CONTRAST

In order to determine how to compare and contrast texts from the same period, and how these texts treat similar themes or topics, use the following steps:

- ✓ first, choose two or more foundational works of American literature written during the eighteenth, nineteenth, or early twentieth centuries
- ✓ next, identify the topic and themes in each work, and any central or recurring ideas the author presents
- ✓ then, explain how each text treats similar themes, including customs, beliefs, and social norms, that reflect the time period in which it was written
- ✓ finally, point out the similarities and differences between the texts, including the themes, topics, and poetic or literary techniques

To compare and contrast eighteenth-, nineteenth-, and early-twentieth-century foundational works of American literature, consider the following questions:

- ✓ What themes and topics are presented in each work?
- ✓ How are the themes or topics in these literary works similar and different?
- ✓ What literary and poetic devices or textual features are used?
- ✓ How are the literary and poetic devices or textual features alike? How are they different?

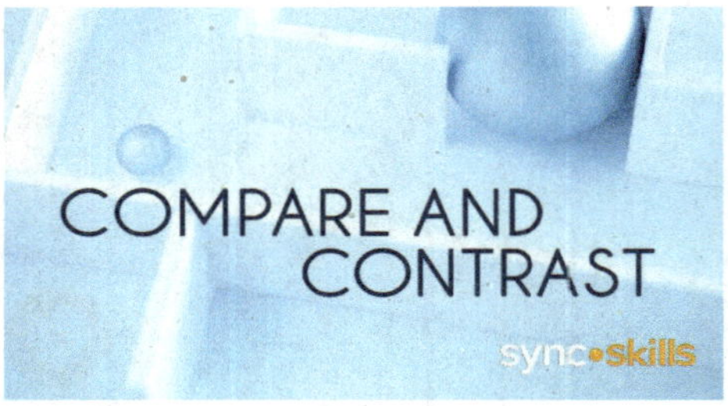

Skill: Compare and Contrast

Reread stanzas 14 through 17 of "An Address to Miss Phillis Wheatley" and the entirety of "On Being Brought from Africa to America." Then, using the Checklist on the previous page, answer the multiple-choice questions below.

YOUR TURN

1. How does each poet describe his or her experience with religion in different ways?

   - O A. Wheatley says that religion turned her away from a "pagan" life, whereas Hammon says it made him feel discriminated against.
   - O B. Wheatley uses religion as a metaphor for her experience, whereas Hammon uses scripture to give his argument credibility.
   - O C. Wheatley views her beliefs as a way to gain acceptance from others, whereas Hammon's beliefs bring him peace and happiness.
   - O D. Wheatley uses less religious imagery in her poem than Hammon does.

2. Since the two poems are autobiographical, which inference about each poet's experience is best supported by comparing and contrasting the language in each text?

   - O A. Both poets seem thankful for their religious experiences in America.
   - O B. Both poets seem angry about their experiences with conversion.
   - O C. Both poets experienced uncertainty about their Christian faith.
   - O D. Both poets use rhyme as a humorous technique in their poems.

Close Read

Reread "An Address to Miss Phillis Wheatley" and "On Being Brought from Africa to America." As you reread, complete the Skills Focus questions below. Then use your answers and annotations from the questions to help you complete the Write activity.

SKILLS FOCUS

1. Identify Hammon's commands in the first three stanzas. What is he advising his reader to do? Cite evidence to support your answer.

2. In her poem "On Being Brought from Africa to America," Wheatley states, "'Twas mercy brought me from my *Pagan* land, / Taught my benighted soul to understand." Explain whether Hammon and Wheatley have similar perspectives. Find evidence from Hammon's poem to support your answer.

3. How do Hammon and Wheatley's relationship with religion support or challenge the concept of independence? Cite evidence from the poems to support your answer.

WRITE

COMPARE AND CONTRAST: Citing clear, supporting evidence from both texts, compare and contrast the overall attitude toward religion in each poem. In which ways do the authors agree about religion, and in which ways do they disagree?

Letters to John Adams

ARGUMENTATIVE TEXT
Abigail Adams
1774, 1776

Introduction

Abigail Adams (1744–1818) was known to the world as the loyal wife of John Adams, second president of the United States, but she actively participated in the events of some of the most tumultuous years of the nation, including the American Revolution. Adams wrote about her experiences in more than 1,100 letters that have endured over time, her words vibrating with personality. She could be unapologetically opinionated, seeking to enlarge her husband's sense of morality on topics like slavery and women's rights. She sent the following letters to her husband while he was serving as a Massachusetts delegate at the Continental Congresses in Philadelphia.

"Remember, all men would be tyrants if they could."

NOTES

Letter to John Adams
September 22, 1774
Boston Garrison, Massachusetts

1 I have just returned from a visit to my Brother, with my Father who carried me there the day before yesterday, and called here in my return to see this much injured Town. I view it with much the same sensations that I should the body of a departed Friend, only put off its present Glory, for to rise finally to a more happy State. I will not despair, but will believe that our cause being good we shall finally prevail. The Maxim 'In time of peace prepare for war' (if this may be called a time of peace) resounds throughout the Country. Next Tuesday they are warned at Braintree all above 15 and under 60 to attend with their arms, and to train once a fortnight from that time, is a Scheme which lays much at heart with many.

2 Scot has arrived, and brings news that he expected to find all peace and Quietness here as he left them at home. You will have more particulars than I am able to send you, from much better hands. There has been in Town a conspiracy of the Negroes. At present it is kept pretty private and was discovered by one who endeavored to dissuade them from it--he being threatened with his life, applied to Justice Quincy for protection. They conducted in this way--got an Irishman to draw up a petition to the Governor telling him they would fight for him provided he would arm them and engage to liberate them if he conquered, and it is said that he attended so much to it as to consult Percy upon it, and one Lieut. Small has been very busy and active. There is but little said, and what Steps they will take in consequence of it I know not. I wish most sincerely there was not a Slave in the province. It always appeared a most **iniquitous** Scheme to me--fight ourselves for what we are daily robbing and plundering from those who have as good a right to freedom as we have. You know my mind upon this Subject.

3 I left all our little ones well, and shall return to them to night. I hope to hear from you by the return of the bearer of this and by Revere. I long for the Day of your return, yet look upon you much safer where you are, but know it will not do for you. Not one action has been brought to this court, no business of

NOTES

any sort in your way. All law ceases, and the Gospel will soon follow, for they are supporters of each other. Adieu. My Father hurries me. Yours most sincerely,

4 Abigail

Letter to John Adams
March 31, 1776
Braintree, Massachusetts

. . .

5 The town in general is left in a better state than we expected, more owing to a **precipitate** flight than any regard to the inhabitants, though some individuals discovered a sense of honor and justice and have left the rent of the houses in which they were for the owners and the furniture unhurt, or if damaged sufficient to make it good.

6 Others have committed abominable ravages. The mansion house of your president[1] is safe and the furniture unhurt, whilst both the house and the furniture of the Solicitor General have fallen a prey to their own merciless party. Surely the very fiends feel a reverential awe for virtue and patriotism, whilst they detest the parricide and traitor.

7 I feel very differently at the approach of spring to which I did a month ago. We knew not then whether we could plant or sow with safety, whether when we had toiled we could reap the fruits of our own industry, whether we should not be driven from the sea coasts to seek shelter in the wilderness, but now we feel as if we might sit under our own vine and eat the good of the land.

8 I feel a *gaiete de coeur* to which before I was a stranger. I think the sun looks brighter, the birds sing more melodiously, and nature put on a more cheerful countenance. We feel a **temporary** peace, and the poor fugitives are returning to their deserted habitations.

9 Though we felicitate ourselves, we sympathize with those who are trembling lest the lot of Boston should be theirs. But they cannot be in similar circumstances unless pusillanimity [cowardliness] and cowardice should take possession of them. They have time and warning given them to see the evil and shun it.—I long to hear that you have declared an independency—and by the way, in the new Code of Laws which I suppose it will be necessary for you to make, I desire you would remember the ladies, and be more generous and

1. **president** referring to John Hancock, president of the Continental Congress. When the British occupied Boston, General William Howe took Hancock's house as his headquarters.

NOTES

favorable to them than your ancestors. Do not put such unlimited power into the hands of the husbands. Remember, all men would be tyrants if they could. If particular care and attention is not paid to the ladies, we are determined to foment a rebellion, and will not hold ourselves bound by any laws in which we have no voice, or representation.

10 That your sex are naturally tyrannical is truth so thoroughly established as to admit no dispute, but such of you as wish to be happy willingly give up the harsh title of master for the more tender and endearing one of friend. Why, then, not put it out of the power of the vicious and the lawless to use us with cruelty and indignity with **impunity.** Men of sense in all ages abhor those customs which treat us only as the **vassals** of your sex. Regard us then as beings placed by providence under your protection, and in imitation of the Supreme Being, make use of that power only for our happiness.

11 Abigail

WRITE

CORRESPONDENCE: Imagine you are Abigail Adams in present day. Using the approach she takes in her letters as an inspiration, write a letter exploring an issue you think Abigail Adams would write about today. Use the format and style of her letters to inform your own.

1776

INFORMATIONAL TEXT
David McCullough
2005

Introduction

Author David McCullough (b. 1933) provides a balanced point of view and new insight into King George III and the American rebels in his book *1776*. McCullough is the highly acclaimed author of more than a dozen historical narratives. Among his many accolades, he is a two-time National Book Award winner and two-time Pulitzer Prize winner. His work brings history to life with vivid detail, historical fact, and rich character portrayals. In this excerpt, he takes us back in time and shows us the American Revolution through the eyes of the British.

"I have no doubt but the nation at large sees the conduct in America in its true light."

NOTES

from Chapter One: Sovereign Duty

1 He had never been a soldier. He had never been to America, any more than he had set foot in Scotland or Ireland. But with absolute certainty he knew what must be done. He would trust to Providence and his high sense of duty. America must be made to obey.

2 "I have no doubt but the nation at large sees the conduct in America in its true light," he had written to his Prime Minister, Lord North, "and I am certain any other conduct but compelling obedience would be ruinous and . . . therefore no consideration could bring me to swerve from the present path which I think myself in duty-bound to follow."

3 In the House of Lords[1] in March of 1775, when challenged on the chances of Britain ever winning a war in America, Lord Sandwich, First Lord of the Admiralty, had looked incredulous. "Suppose the colonies do abound in men, what does that signify?" he asked. "They are raw, undisciplined, cowardly men." And Lord Sandwich was by no means alone in that opinion. General James Grant, a member of the House of Commons[2], had boasted that with 5,000 British regulars he could march from one end of the American continent to the other, a claim that was widely quoted.

4 But in striking contrast, several of the most powerful speakers in Parliament, like the flamboyant Lord Mayor of London, John Wilkes, and the leading Whig intellectual, Edmund Burke, had voiced ardent support for and admiration of the Americans. On March 22, in the House of Commons, Burke had delivered in his heavy Irish brogue one of the longest, most brilliant speeches of his career, calling for conciliation with America.

1. **House of Lords** the upper house of Parliament in the United Kingdom, membership of which is determined by appointment
2. **House of Commons** the lower house of Parliament, consisting of elected officials who meet at the Palace of Westminster

NOTES

5 Yet for all that, no one in either house, Tory[3] or Whig[4], denied the supremacy of Parliament in determining what was best for America. Even Edmund Burke in his celebrated speech had referred repeatedly to "our" colonies.

6 Convinced that his army at Boston was insufficient, the King had dispatched reinforcements and three of his best major generals: William Howe, John Burgoyne, and Henry Clinton. Howe, a member of Parliament and a Whig, had earlier told his Nottingham constituents that if it came to war in America and he were offered a command, he would decline. But now duty called. "I was ordered, and could not refuse, without incurring the **odious** name of backwardness, to serve my country in distress," he explained. Howe, who had served in America during the Seven Years' War[5]—or the French and Indian War, as it was known in America—was convinced the "insurgents" were few in number in comparison to those loyal to the Crown.

7 War had come on April 19, with the first blood shed at Lexington and Concord near Boston, then savagely on June 17 at Breed's Hill and Bunker Hill. (The June engagement was commonly known as the Battle of Bunker Hill on both sides of the Atlantic.) British troops remained under siege at Boston and were running short of food and supplies. On July 3, General George Washington of Virginia had taken command of the American "rabble."

8 With 3,000 miles of ocean separating Britain from her American colonies, accounts of such events took a month or more to reach London. By the time the first news of Lexington and Concord arrived, it was the end of May and Parliament had begun its long summer holiday, its members departing London for their country estates.

9 When the outcome at Bunker Hill became known in the last week of July, it only hardened the King's resolve. "We must persist," he told Lord North. "I know I am doing my duty and therefore can never wish to **retract**."

10 The ever-obliging North suggested that in view of the situation in America, it might no longer be regarded as a rebellion, but as a "foreign war," and thus "every expedient" might be employed.

11 At a hurried meeting at 10 Downing Street, on July 26, the Cabinet decided to send 2,000 reinforcements to Boston without delay and to have an army of no fewer than 20,000 regulars in America by the following spring.

3. **Tory** a member or supporter of the conservative party of the United Kingdom
4. **Whig** Between the 17th and 18th centuries, Tories feuded with Whigs, who espoused liberal ideals and opposition to monarchy.
5. **Seven Years' War** a war between the big European powers in the mid-1700s featuring global battles waged in the Americas, the Philippines, Europe, India, and West Africa

NOTES

12 Bunker Hill was proclaimed a British victory, which technically it was. But in plain truth His Majesty's forces, led by General Howe, had suffered more than 1,000 casualties in an appalling slaughter before gaining the high ground. As was observed acidly in both London and Boston, a few more such victories would surely spell ruin for the victors.

13 At summer's end a British ship out of Boston docked at Plymouth bearing 170 sick and wounded officers and soldiers, most of whom had fought at Bunker Hill and "all in great distress," as described in a vivid published account:

14 A few of the men came on shore, when never hardly were seen such objects: some without legs, and others without arms; and their clothes hanging on them like a loose morning gown, so much were they fallen away by sickness and want of nourishment. There were, moreover, near sixty women and children on board, the widows and children of men who were slain. Some of these too exhibited a most shocking spectacle; and even the vessel itself, though very large, was almost intolerable, from the stench arising from the sick and wounded.

15 The miseries of the troops still besieged at Boston, and of those Americans loyal to the King who, fearing for their lives, had abandoned everything to find refuge in the town, were also described in letters published in the London papers or in correspondence to friends and relatives in London. In the *General Evening Post*, one soldier portrayed the scene in Boston as nothing but "melancholy, disease, and death." Another, whose letter appeared in the *Morning Chronicle and Advertiser*, described being "almost lost for want of fresh provisions . . . . We are entirely blocked up . . . like birds in a cage."

16 John Singleton Copley, the American portrait painter who had left Boston to live in London the year before, read in a letter from his half brother, Henry Pelham:

17 *It is inconceivable the distress and ruin this unnatural dispute has caused to this town and its inhabitants. Almost every shop and store is shut. No business of any kind is going on. . . . I am with the multitude* ***rendered*** *very unhappy, the little I collected entirely lost. The clothes upon my back and a few dollars in my pocket are now the only property which I have.*

18 Despite the war, or more likely because of it, the King remained popular in the country at large and could count on a loyal following in Parliament. Political philosophy, patriotism, and a sense of duty comparable to the King's own figured strongly in both houses. So, too, did the immense patronage and public money that were his alone to dispense. And if that were not sufficient, there was the outright bribery that had become standard in a blatantly **mercenary** system not of his making, but that he readily employed to get his way.

NOTES

19 Indeed, bribery, favoritism, and corruption in a great variety of forms were rampant not only in politics, but at all levels of society. The clergy and such celebrated observers of the era as Jonathan Swift and Tobias Smollett had long since made it a favorite subject. London, said Smollett, was "the devil's drawing-room." Samuel Curwen, the Salem Loyalist, saw dissipation and "vicious indulgence" everywhere he looked, "from the lowest haunts to the most elegant and expensive rendezvous of the noble and polished world." Feeling a touch of homesickness, Curwen thanked God this was still not so back in New England.

20 To much of the press and the opposition in Parliament, the American war and its handling could not have been more misguided. The *Evening Post*, the most **partisan** in its denunciations, called the war "unnatural, unconstitutional, unnecessary, unjust, dangerous, hazardous, and unprofitable." The *St. James's Chronicle* wrote contemptuously of "a foolish, obstinate, and unrelenting King." *The Crisis*, a vehement new paper, attacked "all the gaudy trappings of royalty" and the villainy of the King.

21 "What, in God's name, are ye all about in England? Have you forgot us?" asked a British officer in a letter from Boston published in London's *Morning Chronicle*. He wished that all the "violent people" who favored more vigorous measures in America could be sent over to see for themselves. Their vigor would be quickly cooled.

Excerpted from *1776* by David McCullough, published by Simon and Schuster.

WRITE

PERSONAL RESPONSE: After reading *1776*, do you agree with King George III's decision to go to war? What would you have done to settle the conflict with the colonies, and why? Write an essay explaining your position, supporting your response with evidence from the text.

Declaration of Independence

ARGUMENTATIVE TEXT
Thomas Jefferson
1776

Introduction

On June 11, 1776, the delegates of the Second Continental Congress appointed a committee to draft a statement declaring independence from Britain. The committee included Benjamin Franklin, John Adams, and Thomas Jefferson, who was tasked with putting the committee's ideas to paper, inspired by the English political philosopher John Locke, whose theory of "natural law" states that human beings are "by nature free, equal and independent." Although the Declaration of Independence did not guarantee equality for *all* people, it was a significant first step toward establishing America's democracy.

"We hold these truths to be self-evident, that all men are created equal . . ."

NOTES

Skill: Primary and Secondary Sources

The text begins with the date of writing, showing that this is a primary source because it indicates a time period. The text also says it is a declaration, or first hand account, which makes me think it is a primary source.

Skill: Author's Purpose and Point of View

Jefferson uses specific phrases to indicate that he believes the king has treated the colonies poorly. Based on this treatment, I can infer that Jefferson is critical of the king's behavior.

1 In Congress, July 4, 1776

2 The unanimous Declaration of the thirteen united States of America[1]

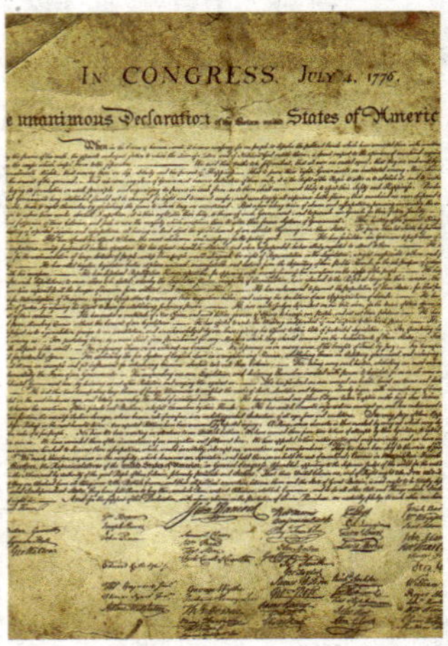

The Declaration of Independence, 1776

3 When in the Course of human events, it becomes necessary for one people to **dissolve** the political bands which have connected them with another, and to assume, among the Powers of the earth, the separate and equal station to which the Laws of Nature and of Nature's God entitle them, a decent respect to the opinions of mankind requires that they should declare the causes which impel them to the separation.

4 We hold these truths to be self-evident, that all men are created equal, that they are endowed by their Creator with certain unalienable Rights, that among these are Life, Liberty, and the pursuit of Happiness.—That to secure these rights, Governments are instituted among Men, deriving their just powers from the consent of the governed,—That whenever any Form of Government becomes destructive of these ends, it is the Right of the People to alter or to abolish it, and to institute new Government, laying its foundation on such principles and organizing its powers in such form, as to them shall seem most likely to effect their Safety and Happiness. Prudence, indeed, will dictate that Governments long established should not be changed for light and transient causes; and accordingly all experience hath shown, that mankind are more disposed to suffer, while evils are sufferable, than to right themselves by abolishing the forms to which they are accustomed. But when a long train of abuses and usurpations, pursuing invariably the same Object evinces a design to reduce them under absolute Despotism, it is their right, it is their duty, to throw off such Government, and to provide new Guards for their future security.—Such has been the patient sufferance of these Colonies;

1. **thirteen united States of America** the original thirteen British colonies on the east coast of America

and such is now the necessity which constrains them to alter their former Systems of Government. The history of the present King of Great Britain[2] is a history of repeated injuries and usurpations, all having in direct object the establishment of an absolute Tyranny over these States. To prove this, let Facts be submitted to a candid world.

5 He has refused his Assent to Laws, the most wholesome and necessary for the public good.

6 He has forbidden his Governors to pass Laws of immediate and pressing importance, unless suspended in their operation till his Assent should be obtained; and when so suspended, he has utterly neglected to attend to them.

7 He has refused to pass other Laws for the accommodation of large districts of people, unless those people would relinquish the right of Representation in the Legislature, a right inestimable to them and formidable to tyrants only.

8 He has called together legislative bodies at places unusual, uncomfortable, and distant from the depository of their Public Records, for the sole purpose of fatiguing them into compliance with his measures.

9 He has dissolved Representative Houses[3] repeatedly, for opposing with manly firmness his invasions on the rights of the people.

10 He has refused for a long time, after such dissolutions, to cause others to be elected; whereby the Legislative Powers, incapable of Annihilation, have returned to the People at large for their exercise; the State remaining in the mean time exposed to all the dangers of invasion from without, and convulsions within.

11 He has endeavoured to prevent the population of these States; for that purpose obstructing the Laws of Naturalization of Foreigners; refusing to pass others to encourage their migration hither, and raising the conditions of new Appropriations of Lands.

12 He has obstructed the Administration of Justice, by refusing his Assent to Laws for establishing Judiciary Powers.

13 He has made judges dependent on his Will alone, for the tenure of their offices, and the amount and payment of their salaries.

NOTES

Skill: Rhetoric

Jefferson repeats "He has" to show a pattern of offenses committed by King George III. Jefferson uses the rhetorical device of repetition to emphasize the number of ways that the colonies have been mistreated.

2. **King of Great Britain** King George III, whose exceptionally long reign over Britain and Ireland was marked by military conflict
3. **Representative Houses** organizations designed to give American colonists a voice in the British government

NOTES

14 He has erected a multitude of New Offices, and sent hither swarms of Officers to harass our People, and eat out their substance.

15 He has kept among us, in times of peace, Standing Armies without the Consent of our legislatures.

16 He has affected to render the Military independent of and superior to the Civil Power.

17 He has combined with others to subject us to a **jurisdiction** foreign to our constitution, and unacknowledged by our laws; giving his Assent to their Acts of pretended legislation:

18 For quartering large bodies of armed troops among us:

19 For protecting them, by a mock Trial, from Punishment for any Murders which they should commit on the Inhabitants of these States:

20 For cutting off our Trade with all parts of the world:

21 For imposing taxes on us without our Consent:

22 For depriving us, in many cases, of the benefits of Trial by Jury:

23 For transporting us beyond Seas to be tried for pretended offences:

24 For abolishing the free System of English Laws in a neighbouring Province, establishing therein an Arbitrary government, and enlarging its Boundaries so as to render it at once an example and fit instrument for introducing the same absolute rule into these Colonies:

25 For taking away our Charters, abolishing our most valuable Laws, and altering fundamentally the Forms of our Governments:

26 For suspending our own Legislatures and declaring themselves invested with Power to legislate for us in all cases whatsoever.

27 He has abdicated Government here, by declaring us out of his Protection and waging War against us.

28 He has plundered our seas, ravaged our Coasts, burnt our towns, and destroyed the lives of our people.

NOTES

29 He is at this time transporting large armies of foreign mercenaries to complete the works of death, desolation and tyranny, already begun with circumstances of Cruelty & perfidy scarcely paralleled in the most barbarous ages, and totally unworthy of the Head of a civilized nation.

30 He has constrained our fellow Citizens taken Captive on the high Seas to bear Arms against their Country, to become the executioners of their friends and Brethren, or to fall themselves by their Hands.

31 He has excited domestic insurrections amongst us, and has endeavoured to bring on the inhabitants of our frontiers, the merciless Indian Savages, whose known rule of warfare is an undistinguished destruction of all ages, sexes and conditions.

32 In every stage of these Oppressions We have Petitioned for Redress in the most humble terms: Our repeated Petitions have been answered only by repeated injury. A Prince, whose character is thus marked by every act which may define a Tyrant, is unfit to be the ruler of a free People.

33 Nor have We been wanting in attention to our British brethren. We have warned them from time to time of attempts by their legislature to extend an unwarrantable jurisdiction over us. We have reminded them of the circumstances of our emigration and settlement here. We have appealed to their native justice and **magnanimity,** and we have conjured them by the ties of our common kindred to disavow these usurpations, which would inevitably interrupt our connections and correspondence. They too have been deaf to the voice of justice and of **consanguinity**. We must, therefore, acquiesce in the necessity, which denounces our Separation, and hold them, as we hold the rest of mankind, Enemies in War, in Peace Friends.

34 We, therefore, the Representatives of the United States of America, in General Congress, Assembled, appealing to the Supreme Judge of the world for the **rectitude** of our intentions, do, in the Name, and by the Authority of the good People of these Colonies, solemnly publish and declare, That these United Colonies are, and of Right ought to be Free and Independent States; that they are Absolved from all Allegiance to the British Crown, and that all political connection between them and the State of Great Britain, is and ought to be totally dissolved; and that as Free and Independent States, they have full Power to levy War, conclude Peace, contract Alliances, establish Commerce, and to do all other Acts and Things which Independent States may of right do. And for the support of this Declaration, with a firm reliance on the Protection of Divine Providence, we mutually pledge to each other our Lives, our Fortunes and our sacred Honor.

First Read

Read the Declaration of Independence. After you read, complete the Think Questions below.

THINK QUESTIONS

1. According to paragraph 3, what is the purpose of the Declaration of Independence beyond simply claiming freedom from British rule? Identify the phrase that states this purpose most clearly and relate it to the rest of the document.

2. In paragraph 4, what does Jefferson say about the treatment of the colonists under the king of Great Britain? According to Jefferson, what justifies a revolt against the existing government? Use evidence from the text to support your response.

3. Where in the document does Jefferson officially declare independence, and how does he define independence for the colonies? Use evidence from the text to support your response.

4. The Latin prefix *con-* means "with." The Latin root *sanguis* means "blood." Using this information and your knowledge of word patterns and relationships, write your best definition of the word **consanguinity** here.

5. The Latin root *rect* means "right" or "straight." With this information in mind and using context clues from the text, write your best definition of the word **rectitude** here. Then verify your meaning using a print or digital dictionary.

Skill: Author's Purpose and Point of View

Use the Checklist to analyze Author's Purpose and Point of View in the Declaration of Independence. Refer to the sample student annotations about Author's Purpose and Point of View in the text.

••• CHECKLIST LIST FOR AUTHOR'S PURPOSE AND POINT OF VIEW

In order to identify author's purpose and point of view, note the following:

- ✓ whether the writer is attempting to establish trust by citing his or her experience or education
- ✓ whether the evidence the author provides is convincing and whether the argument or position is logical
- ✓ what words and phrases the author uses to appeal to the emotions
- ✓ the author's use of rhetoric, or the art of speaking and writing persuasively, such as the use of repetition to drive home a point as well as allusion and alliteration
- ✓ the author's use of rhetoric to contribute to the power, persuasiveness, or beauty of the text

To determine the author's purpose and point of view, consider the following questions:

- ✓ How does the author try to convince me that he or she has something valid and important for me to read?
- ✓ What words or phrases express emotion or invite an emotional response? How or why are they effective or ineffective?
- ✓ What words and phrases contribute to the power, persuasiveness, or beauty of the text? Is the author's use of rhetoric successful? Why or why not?

Skill: Author's Purpose and Point of View

Reread paragraphs 27–31 from the Declaration of Independence. Then, using the Checklist on the previous page, answer the multiple-choice questions below.

YOUR TURN

1. What is Jefferson's purpose for listing all of the colonists' grievances against the king?

   ○ A. to show the audience that he keeps very meticulous records of events
   ○ B. to introduce his argument for independence
   ○ C. to share a personal experience in support of the argument for independence
   ○ D. to persuade the audience that they have just cause for choosing independence

2. Words such as "plundered," "ravaged," and "destroyed" support the idea that Jefferson's attitude towards the king is—

   ○ A. understanding.
   ○ B. hostile.
   ○ C. frustrated.
   ○ D. critical.

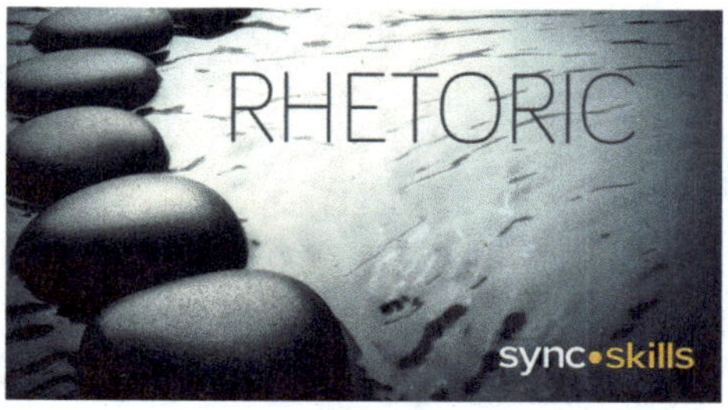

Skill: Rhetoric

Use the Checklist to analyze Rhetoric in the Declaration of Independence. Refer to the sample student annotations about Rhetoric in the text.

••• CHECKLIST FOR RHETORIC

In order to identify an author's point of view or purpose in a text and to analyze the rhetoric of the text, note the following:

- ✓ the purpose of the text
- ✓ details and statements that identify the author's point of view or purpose
- ✓ when the author uses rhetoric to advance his or her point of view or purpose. Rhetoric is the way by which writers phrase, or construct, what they want to say. Writers use many different kinds of rhetorical devices, and the style they employ can contribute to the power, persuasiveness, or beauty of the text. Look for:
    - an author's use of sensory language
    - words that appeal to the senses, which can create a vivid picture in the minds of readers and listeners and persuade them to accept a specific point of view
    - a specific style, such as the use of assonance or the repetition of certain words, which can be used to create catchphrases, phrases that can be widely or repeatedly used and that can be easily remembered
- ✓ when the author's use of rhetoric is particularly effective

To determine an author's point of view or purpose in a text in which the rhetoric is particularly effective, consider the following questions:

- ✓ Which rhetorical devices can you identify in the text?
- ✓ How does this writer or speaker use rhetorical devices to persuade an audience?
- ✓ Do the rhetorical devices work to make the argument or position sound? Why or why not?
- ✓ How does the use of rhetorical devices affect the way the text is read and understood?
- ✓ In what ways are the rhetorical devices particularly effective?

Skill: Rhetoric

Reread paragraph 33 from the Declaration of Independence. Then, using the Checklist on the previous page, answer the multiple-choice questions below.

YOUR TURN

1. The repetition of the phrase "We have" at the beginning of many sentences serves to—

   - O A. provide a rhetorical shift for Jefferson to change topics.
   - O B. appeal to readers' emotions about seeking independence.
   - O C. emphasize the actions the colonists took to communicate and reason with the British.
   - O D. offer an antithesis to the rest of Jefferson's argument about Britain's leadership.

2. The logical presentation of facts in this paragraph leads Jefferson to conclude that—

   - O A. going to war is always the best way to solve problems.
   - O B. there is hope for reconciliation with British leadership.
   - O C. the British will be shocked by the complaints outlined in the Declaration.
   - O D. the cause of independence is more important than past relationships.

Skill:
Primary and Secondary Sources

Use the Checklist to analyze Primary and Secondary Sources in the Declaration of Independence. Refer to the sample student annotations about Primary and Secondary Sources in the text.

••• CHECKLIST FOR PRIMARY AND SECONDARY SOURCES

In order to differentiate between primary and secondary sources, do the following:

- ✓ examine the source, noting the title, author, and date of publication
- ✓ identify the genre of the source
  - Primary sources include letters, diaries, journals, speeches, eyewitness interviews, oral histories, memoirs, and autobiographies.
  - Secondary sources include encyclopedia articles, newspaper and magazine articles, biographies, documentary films, history books, and textbooks.

If the source meets one or more of the following criteria, it is considered a primary source:

- ✓ original, first-hand account of an event or time period
- ✓ writing that takes place during the event or time period

If the source meets one or more of the following criteria, it is considered a secondary source:

- ✓ a book or an article that analyzes and interprets primary sources
- ✓ a second-hand account of a historical event
- ✓ a book or an article that interprets or analyzes creative work

To analyze seventeenth-, eighteenth-, and nineteenth-century foundational U.S. documents of historical and literary significance, consider the following questions:

- ✓ How is the source reliable and credible?
- ✓ What is the purpose of this source?
- ✓ What historical themes, such as patriotism or heroism, are brought out in the source?
- ✓ How does the author use anecdotes, interviews, allusions, or other rhetorical features?
- ✓ What gives this source literary or historical significance?

Skill: Primary and Secondary Sources

Reread paragraph 34 from the Declaration of Independence. Then, using the Checklist on the previous page, answer the multiple-choice questions below.

YOUR TURN

1. This question has two parts. First, answer Part A. Then, answer Part B.

   Part A: What early American values are emphasized in the closing of this document?

   - A. isolation and exclusion
   - B. participation in government and civic affairs
   - C. peace and prosperity
   - D. freedom and independence

   Part B: Which line from the passage best supports your answer in Part A?

   - A. "appealing to the Supreme Judge of the world for the rectitude of our intentions"
   - B. "That these United Colonies are, and of Right ought to be Free and Independent States"
   - C. "all political connection between them and the State of Great Britain, is and ought to be totally dissolved"
   - D. "with a firm reliance on the Protection of Divine Providence, we mutually pledge to each other our Lives, our Fortunes and our sacred Honor"

2. What gives this text historical significance?

   - A. It illustrates the government structures in place at the time of its writing.
   - B. It marks the transition from colonies to independent states, and the founding of our nation.
   - C. It is an important reminder of Great Britain's treatment of the colonies.
   - D. It is an example of how to make a strong argument.

Close Read

Reread the Declaration of Independence. As you reread, complete the Skills Focus questions below. Then use your answers and annotations from the questions to help you complete the Write activity.

SKILLS FOCUS

1. What is Thomas Jefferson's point of view regarding the relationship between the colonies and the king? Identify evidence that demonstrates his attitude.

2. Identify Jefferson's call to action as he addresses his audience in the final paragraphs of this text. What is his purpose as a writer?

3. The repetition of a word or phrase is a kind of rhetorical device. Identify an example of the repetition of a word or phrase in the text, and analyze its effectiveness in persuading readers to support the claim.

4. How does this document highlight important American values? Identify examples throughout the text.

5. The ways in which Britain controlled the colonies influenced the laws and system of government that the Founding Fathers put into place. Find examples of specific grievances against the king that Jefferson cites, and explain how our Constitution prevents such abuses.

WRITE

RHETORICAL ANALYSIS: In addition to setting out the goals of a new nation, the Declaration of Independence also inspired colonists to join the Revolutionary cause. Explain how the document uses rhetoric to make its message more compelling, and determine which arguments are most relevant to American society today. Be sure to cite evidence from the text to support your response.

The Whistle

INFORMATIONAL TEXT
Benjamin Franklin
1779

Introduction

Benjamin Franklin (1706–1790) was a scientist, writer, publisher, inventor, statesman, musician, philosopher, and Founding Father of the United States. A gifted and prolific storyteller, Benjamin Franklin drew upon incidents from his boyhood in Boston to illustrate and examine morality. Some of his writings are collected in *Poor Richard's Almanack*, a yearly publication Franklin wrote, compiled, and published for more than 25 years. The following letter, written to a friend in 1779, contains elements of the humor and integrity that mark Franklin's unique style.

". . . we should draw all the good we can from this world."

NOTES

To Madame Brillon,

1 . . . I am charmed with your description of Paradise, and with your plan of living there; and I approve much of your conclusion, that, in the meantime, we should draw all the good we can from this world. In my opinion we might all draw more good from it than we do, and suffer less evil, if we would take care not to give too much for whistles. For to me it seems that most of the unhappy people we meet with are become so by neglect of that caution.

2 You ask what I mean? You love stories, and will excuse my telling one of myself.

3 When I was a child of seven years old, my friends, on a holiday, filled my pocket with coppers. I went directly to a shop where they sold toys for children; and being charmed with the sound of a whistle, that I met by the way in the hands of another boy, I voluntarily offered and gave all my money for one. I then came home, and went whistling all over the house, much pleased with my whistle, but disturbing all the family. My brothers, and sisters, and cousins, understanding the bargain I had made, told me I had given four times as much for it as it was worth; put me in mind what good things I might have bought with the rest of the money; and laughed at me so much for my folly, that I cried with vexation; and the **reflection** gave me more **chagrin** than the whistle gave me pleasure.

Skill: Informational Text Elements

Franklin's telling a story within his letter to explain what he meant about the whistle. The story helps support his primary goal for writing.

4 This, however, was afterwards of use to me, the impression continuing on my mind; so that often, when I was tempted to buy some unnecessary thing, I said to myself, Don't give too much for the whistle; and I saved my money.

5 As I grew up, came into the world, and observed the actions of men, I thought I met with many, very many, who gave too much for the whistle.

6 When I saw one too ambitious of court favor, sacrificing his time in attendance on levees[1], his repose, his liberty, his virtue, and perhaps his friends, to attain it, I have said to myself, this man gives too much for his whistle.

1. **in attendance on levees** in Franklin's time, a *levee* was a formal reception or assembly of visitors

NOTES

7 When I saw another fond of popularity, constantly employing himself in political bustles, neglecting his own affairs, and ruining them by that neglect, "He pays, indeed," said I, "too much for his whistle."

8 If I knew a miser, who gave up every kind of comfortable living, all the pleasure of doing good to others, all the esteem of his fellow-citizens, and the joys of **benevolent** friendship, for the sake of accumulating wealth, "Poor man," said I, "you pay too much for your whistle."

9 When I met with a man of pleasure, sacrificing every **laudable** improvement of the mind, or of his fortune, to mere **corporeal** sensations, and ruining his health in their pursuit, "Mistaken man," said I, "you are providing pain for yourself, instead of pleasure; you give too much for your whistle."

10 If I see one fond of appearance, or fine clothes, fine houses, fine furniture, fine equipages, all above his fortune, for which he contracts debts, and ends his career in a prison, "Alas!" say I, "he has paid dear, very dear, for his whistle."

11 When I see a beautiful sweet-tempered girl married to an ill-natured brute of a husband, "What a pity," say I, "that she should pay so much for a whistle!"

12 In short, I conceive that great part of the miseries of mankind are brought upon them by the false estimates they have made of the value of things, and by their giving too much for their whistles.

13 Yet I ought to have charity for these unhappy people, when I consider that, with all this wisdom of which I am boasting, there are certain things in the world so tempting, for example, the apples of King John, which happily are not to be bought; for if they were put to sale by auction, I might very easily be led to ruin myself in the purchase, and find that I had once more given too much for the whistle.

14 Adieu, my dear friend, and believe me ever yours very sincerely and with unalterable affection.

First Read

Read “The Whistle.” After you read, complete the Think Questions below.

THINK QUESTIONS

1. Why does the author begin his letter with an out of context reference to a whistle? Why doesn’t he just tell his anecdote outright? Use evidence from the text to support your response.

2. What childhood event upset Franklin so much that he “cried with vexation”? Why was he so upset? Use specific details from the text to support your answer.

3. How does Franklin connect the characters of the miser, the man of pleasure, and the man who is fond of appearance? Refer to evidence in the text to support your response.

4. Use context clues to determine the meaning of the word **chagrin** as it is used in the text. Write your definition of *chagrin* here, along with those words or phrases from the text that helped you determine its meaning.

5. The Latin word *bene* means “well” and the Latin word *velle* means “to wish.” With this information in mind and using context clues from the text, write your best definition of the word **benevolent** here.

Skill: Informational Text Elements

Use the Checklist to analyze Informational Text Elements in "The Whistle." Refer to the sample student annotations about Informational Text Elements in the text.

••• CHECKLIST FOR INFORMATIONAL TEXT ELEMENTS

In order to identify a complex set of ideas or sequence of events, note the following:

- ✓ key details in the text that provide information about individuals, events, and ideas
- ✓ interactions between specific individuals, ideas, or events
- ✓ important developments over the course of the text
- ✓ transition words and phrases that signal interactions between individuals, events, and ideas, such as *because*, *as a consequence*, or *as a result*
- ✓ similarities and differences of types of information in a text

To analyze a complex set of ideas or sequence of events and explain how specific individuals, ideas, or events interact and develop over the course of the text, consider the following questions:

- ✓ How does the author present the information as a sequence of events?
- ✓ How does the order in which ideas or events are presented affect the connections between them?
- ✓ How do specific individuals, ideas, or events interact and develop over the course of the text?
- ✓ What other features, if any, help readers to analyze the events, ideas, or individuals in the text?

Skill: Informational Text Elements

Reread paragraph 13 of "The Whistle." Then, using the Checklist on the previous page, answer the multiple-choice questions below.

YOUR TURN

1. This question has two parts. First, answer Part A. Then, answer Part B.

Part A: What is most likely Franklin's purpose for including this paragraph in the letter?

- O A. To demonstrate that he also feels sorry for boastful people.
- O B. To demonstrate that he would be happier if he "gave too much for the whistle."
- O C. To demonstrate that he has been ruined by the lesson.
- O D. To demonstrate that he is imperfect and might still "give too much for the whistle."

Part B: Which sentence or phrase from the passage best supports the answer from Part A?

- O A. "with all this wisdom I am boasting . . ."
- O B. "I ought to have charity for these unhappy people . . ."
- O C. "the apples of King John, which happily are not to be bought . . ."
- O D. "I might very easily be led to ruin myself in the purchase . . ."

Close Read

Reread "The Whistle." As you reread, complete the Skills Focus questions below. Then use your answers and annotations from the questions to help you complete the Write activity.

SKILLS FOCUS

1. Identify Franklin's repetition about "the whistle" and explain how it enhances his argument in the letter.

2. Identify the sections of the text about people who have "paid too much for their whistles" and explain what effect the internal structure of these paragraphs has on the reader.

3. Parallelism is the use of a series of words, phrases, or sentences that have similar grammatical structure. Highlight examples of grammatical parallelism in the text. Explain how Franklin's use of parallelism as a rhetorical device emphasizes his points.

4. How might the advice presented in "The Whistle" ensure independence? Highlight an example in the text that reflects the concept of independence most strongly, and explain the ways in which it demonstrates the American spirit.

WRITE

EXPLANATORY: Does Benjamin Franklin's advice have any bearing on your own life? Write a biographical account explaining a time in which you or someone you know "paid too much for a whistle." Use informational text elements, such as relevant details, evidence, and conclusion, to develop your account.

The Interesting Narrative of the Life of Olaudah Equiano, or Gustavus Vassa, the African

INFORMATIONAL TEXT

Olaudah Equiano

1789

Introduction

The life of Olaudah Equiano (ca. 1745–1797) was a mixture of tragedy, struggle, and achievement. When Equiano was eleven, he was kidnapped by slave traders in Africa and forced onto a ship to the Caribbean. What he witnessed on board the slave ship haunted him for the rest of his life. Eventually, Equiano was able to purchase his freedom and settle in England, where he became an ardent abolitionist. His greatest contribution to the antislavery movement was his autobiography, in which he provided graphic and powerful descriptions of the inhumanity he and other enslaved people suffered.

"Must every tender feeling be likewise sacrificed to your avarice?"

NOTES

1 The first object which saluted my eyes when I arrived on the coast was the sea, and a slave ship, which was then riding at anchor, and waiting for its cargo. These filled me with astonishment, which was soon converted into terror when I was carried on board. I was immediately handled and tossed up to see if I were sound by some of the crew; and I was now persuaded that I had gotten into a world of bad spirits, and that they were going to kill me.

2 Their complexions too differing so much from ours, their long hair, and the language they spoke, (which was very different from any I had ever heard) united to confirm me in this belief. Indeed such were the horrors of my views and fears at the moment, that, if ten thousand worlds had been my own, I would have freely parted with them all to have exchanged my condition with that of the meanest slave in my own country. When I looked round the ship too and saw a large furnace of copper boiling, and a multitude of black people of every description chained together, every one of their countenances expressing dejection and sorrow, I no longer doubted of my fate; and, quite overpowered with horror and anguish, I fell motionless on the deck and fainted.

3 When I recovered a little I found some black people about me, who I believed were some of those who brought me on board, and had been receiving their pay; they talked to me in order to cheer me, but all in vain. I asked them if we were not to be eaten by those white men with horrible looks, red faces, and loose hair. They told me I was not; and one of the crew brought me a small portion of spirituous liquor in a wine glass; but, being afraid of him, I would not take it out of his hand. One of the blacks therefore took it from him and gave it to me, and I took a little down my palate, which, instead of reviving me, as they thought it would, threw me into the greatest **consternation** at the strange feeling it produced, having never tasted any such liquor before. Soon after this the blacks who brought me on board went off, and left me abandoned to despair.

4 I now saw myself deprived of all chance of returning to my native country, or even the least glimpse of hope of gaining the shore, which I now considered as friendly; and I even wished for my former slavery in preference to my present situation, which was filled with horrors of every kind, still heightened by my ignorance of what I was to undergo. I was not long suffered to indulge my grief;

NOTES

I was soon put down under the decks, and there I received such a salutation in my nostrils as I had never experienced in my life: so that, with the **loathsomeness** of the stench, and crying together, I became so sick and low that I was not able to eat, nor had I the least desire to taste any thing. I now wished for the last friend, death, to relieve me; but soon, to my grief, two of the white men offered me eatables; and, on my refusing to eat, one of them held me fast by the hands, and laid me across I think the windlass, and tied my feet, while the other flogged me severely. I had never experienced any thing of this kind before; and although, not being used to the water, I naturally feared that element the first time I saw it, yet nevertheless, could I have got over the nettings, I would have jumped over the side, but I could not; and, besides, the crew used to watch us very closely who were not chained down to the decks, lest we should leap into the water: and I have seen some of these poor African prisoners most severely cut for attempting to do so, and hourly whipped for not eating. This indeed was often the case with myself. In a little time after, amongst the poor chained men, I found some of my own nation, which in a small degree gave ease to my mind. I inquired of these what was to be done with us; they gave me to understand we were to be carried to these white people's country to work for them. I then was a little revived, and thought, if it were no worse than working, my situation was not so desperate: but still I feared I should be put to death, the white people looked and acted, as I thought, in so savage a manner; for I had never seen among any people such instances of brutal cruelty; and this not only shewn towards us blacks, but also to some of the whites themselves. One white man in particular I saw, when we were permitted to be on deck, flogged so unmercifully with a large rope near the foremast, that he died in consequence of it; and they tossed him over the side as they would have done a brute. This made me fear these people the more; and I expected nothing less than to be treated in the same manner. I could not help expressing my fears and **apprehensions** to some of my countrymen: I asked them if these people had no country, but lived in this hollow place (the ship): they told me they did not, but came from a distant one. 'Then,' said I, 'how comes it in all our country we never heard of them?' They told me because they lived so very far off. I then asked where were their women? had they any like themselves? I was told they had: 'and why,' said I, 'do we not see them?' they answered, because they were left behind. I asked how the vessel could go? they told me they could not tell; but that there were cloths put upon the masts by the help of the ropes I saw, and then the vessel went on; and the white men had some spell or magic they put in the water when they liked in order to stop the vessel. I was exceedingly amazed at this account, and really thought they were spirits. I therefore wished much to be from amongst them, for I expected they would sacrifice me: but my wishes were vain; for we were so quartered that it was impossible for any of us to make our escape.

5 While we stayed on the coast I was mostly on deck; and one day, to my great astonishment, I saw one of these vessels coming in with the sails up. As soon as the whites saw it, they gave a great shout, at which we were amazed; and the

NOTES

more so as the vessel appeared larger by approaching nearer. At last she came to an anchor in my sight, and when the anchor was let go I and my countrymen who saw it were lost in astonishment to observe the vessel stop; and were not convinced it was done by magic. Soon after this the other ship got her boats out, and they came on board of us, and the people of both ships seemed very glad to see each other. Several of the strangers also shook hands with us black people, and made motions with their hands, signifying I suppose we were to go to their country; but we did not understand them.

6 At last, when the ship we were in had got in all her cargo, they made ready with many fearful noises, and we were all put under deck, so that we could not see how they managed the vessel. But this disappointment was the least of my sorrow. The stench of the hold while we were on the coast was so intolerably loathsome, that it was dangerous to remain there for any time, and some of us had been permitted to stay on the deck for the fresh air; but now that the whole ship's cargo were confined together, it became absolutely pestilential. The closeness of the place, and the heat of the climate, added to the number in the ship, which was so crowded that each had scarcely room to turn himself, almost suffocated us. This produced copious perspirations, so that the air soon became unfit for respiration, from a variety of loathsome smells, and brought on a sickness among the slaves, of which many died, thus falling victims to the improvident **avarice**, as I may call it, of their purchasers. This wretched situation was again aggravated by the galling of the chains, now become insupportable; and the filth of the necessary tubs, into which the children often fell, and were almost suffocated. The shrieks of the women, and the groans of the dying, rendered the whole a scene of horror almost inconceivable. Happily perhaps for myself I was soon reduced so low here that it was thought necessary to keep me almost always on deck; and from my extreme youth I was not put in fetters. In this situation I expected every hour to share the fate of my companions, some of whom were almost daily brought upon deck at the point of death, which I began to hope would soon put an end to my miseries. Often did I think many of the inhabitants of the deep much more happy than myself. I envied them the freedom they enjoyed, and as often wished I could change my condition for theirs. Every circumstance I met with served only to render my state more painful, and heighten my apprehensions, and my opinion of the cruelty of the whites.

7 One day they had taken a number of fishes; and when they had killed and satisfied themselves with as many as they thought fit, to our astonishment who were on the deck, rather than give any of them to us to eat as we expected, they tossed the remaining fish into the sea again, although we begged and prayed for some as well as we could, but in vain; and some of my countrymen, being pressed by hunger, took an opportunity, when they thought no one saw them, of trying to get a little privately; but they were discovered, and the attempt procured them some very severe floggings. One day, when we had a smooth sea and moderate wind, two of my wearied

NOTES

countrymen who were chained together (I was near them at the time), preferring death to such a life of misery, somehow made through the nettings and jumped into the sea: immediately another quite dejected fellow, who, on account of his illness, was suffered to be out of irons, also followed their example; and I believe many more would very soon have done the same if they had not been prevented by the ship's crew, who were instantly alarmed. Those of us that were the most active were in a moment put down under the deck, and there was such a noise and confusion amongst the people of the ship as I never heard before, to stop her, and get the boat out to go after the slaves. However two of the wretches were drowned, but they got the other, and afterwards flogged him unmercifully for thus attempting to prefer death to slavery. In this manner we continued to undergo more hardships than I can now relate, hardships which are inseparable from this accursed trade. Many a time we were near suffocation from the want of fresh air, which we were often without for whole days together. This, and the stench of the necessary tubs, carried off many.

8 During our passage I first saw flying fishes, which surprised me very much: they used frequently to fly across the ship, and many of them fell on the deck. I also now first saw the use of the quadrant; I had often with astonishment seen the mariners make observations with it, and I could not think what it meant. They at last took notice of my surprise; and one of them, willing to increase it, as well as to gratify my curiosity, made me one day look through it. The clouds appeared to me to be land, which disappeared as they passed along. This heightened my wonder; and I was now more persuaded than ever that I was in another world, and that every thing about me was magic. At last we came in sight of the island of Barbadoes, at which the whites on board gave a great shout, and made many signs of joy to us. We did not know what to think of this; but as the vessel drew nearer we plainly saw the harbour, and other ships of different kinds and sizes; and we soon anchored amongst them off Bridge Town. Many merchants and planters now came on board, though it was in the evening. They put us in separate parcels, and examined us attentively. They also made us jump, and pointed to the land, signifying we were to go there. We thought by this we should be eaten by these ugly men, as they appeared to us; and, when soon after we were all put down under the deck again, there was much dread and trembling among us, and nothing but bitter cries to be heard all the night from these apprehensions, insomuch that at last the white people got some old slaves from the land to pacify us. They told us we were not to be eaten, but to work, and were soon to go on land, where we should see many of our country people. This report eased us much; and sure enough, soon after we were landed, there came to us Africans of all languages.

9 We were conducted immediately to the merchant's yard, where we were all pent up together like so many sheep in a fold, without regard to sex or age. As every object was new to me every thing I saw filled me with surprise. What struck me first was that the houses were built with stories, and in every other

NOTES

respect different from those in Africa: but I was still more astonished on seeing people on horseback. I did not know what this could mean; and indeed I thought these people were full of nothing but magical arts. While I was in this astonishment one of my fellow prisoners spoke to a countryman of his about the horses, who said they were the same kind they had in their country. I understood them, though they were from a distant part of Africa, and I thought it odd I had not seen any horses there; but afterwards, when I came to converse with different Africans, I found they had many horses amongst them, and much larger than those I then saw.

10 We were not many days in the merchant's custody before we were sold after their usual manner, which is this:—On a signal given, (as the beat of a drum) the buyers rush at once into the yard where the slaves are confined, and make choice of that parcel they like best. The noise and clamour with which this is attended, and the eagerness visible in the countenances of the buyers, serve not a little to increase the apprehensions of the terrified Africans, who may well be supposed to consider them as the ministers of that destruction to which they think themselves devoted. In this manner, without scruple, are relations and friends separated, most of them never to see each other again. I remember in the vessel in which I was brought over, in the men's apartment, there were several brothers, who, in the sale, were sold in different lots; and it was very moving on this occasion to see and hear their cries at parting. O, ye nominal Christians! might not an African ask you, learned you this from your God, who says unto you, Do unto all men as you would men should do unto you? Is it not enough that we are torn from our country and friends to toil for your luxury and lust of gain? Must every tender feeling be likewise sacrificed to your avarice? Are the dearest friends and relations, now rendered more dear by their separation from their kindred, still to be parted from each other, and thus prevented from cheering the gloom of slavery with the small comfort of being together and mingling their sufferings and sorrows? Why are parents to lose their children, brothers their sisters, or husbands their wives? Surely this is a new refinement in cruelty, which, while it has no advantage to **atone** for it, thus aggravates distress, and adds fresh horrors even to the wretchedness of slavery.

WRITE

DISCUSSION: *The Interesting Narrative of the Life of Olaudah Equiano, or Gustavus Vassa, the African* is both a description of the horrors of the Middle Passage and a passionate argument against slavery. What kind of rhetorical devices and appeals does Equiano use at the end of the last paragraph? How do the descriptions throughout the excerpt lend power to Equiano's ultimate argument that the cruel and inhumane separation of families "adds fresh horrors even to the wretchedness of slavery"? Be sure to support your response with evidence from the text.

Extended Writing Project and Grammar

Narrative Writing Process: Plan

PLAN | DRAFT | REVISE | EDIT AND PUBLISH

The story of America is built on the concept of liberty—that we have the right to act and speak as we choose. This belief led to our independence and has continued to influence the course of events in the centuries that have followed, shaping us into the country—and the people—that we are today.

WRITING PROMPT

How does the desire for independence affect our choices?

Write about a character, real or imagined, who feels trapped by circumstance and who wishes to become more independent. Using the skills you have learned in this unit, write a narrative in which a character moves from dependence to independence. Be sure to describe how the character feels limited at the beginning, the decisions the character makes to become independent, and the consequences and responsibilities of this newfound independence. If you choose to write a personal narrative, use the same outline to write about how you or someone you know has achieved independence. Remember to include the following in your narrative:

- a plot with a beginning, a middle, and an end
- a clear setting
- characters and dialogue
- descriptive details
- a clear theme

Introduction to Narrative Writing

Narrative writing tells a story of experiences or events that have been imagined by a writer or that have happened in real life. Good narrative writing effectively uses genre characteristics and craft, such as relevant descriptive details and a purposeful structure with a series of events that includes a beginning, a middle, and an end. The characteristics of narrative writing include:

- setting
- characters
- plot
- theme/ reflection
- point of view

In addition to these characteristics, narrative writers carefully craft their work through their use of dialogue, details, word choice, and figurative language. These choices help to shape the tone, mood, and overall style of the text. Effective narratives combine these genre characteristics and craft to engage the reader.

As you continue with this Extended Writing Project, you'll receive more instruction and practice in crafting each of the characteristics of narrative writing to create your own personal or fictional narrative.

Before you get started on your own fictional or personal narrative, read this narrative that one student, Daniel, wrote in response to the writing prompt. As you read the Model, highlight and annotate the features of narrative writing that Daniel included in his narrative.

NOTES

STUDENT MODEL

The Price of Freedom

1 Nora firmly presses her phone between her ear and shoulder. "I can't believe this is our last summer at camp," she says as she digs through her dirty laundry hamper. "Simone, I have to put you on speaker phone." She sets her phone on the carpet. "Did you borrow my wool socks? I can't find them anywhere."

2 "Nope," Simone replies. Nora sighs. Wool socks are a must-have for cold nights camping in the mountains. Camp doesn't start until a month from now, but she's already packing.

3 "We must make the most out of camp this year. This is our last summer before our senior year! Then comes college, marriage, kids . . . ," Simone hesitates. "Who knows if we'll ever be free of responsibility again?"

4 "No!" Nora cries. "Please don't get serious again. We are still kids! This summer will be the best yet."

5 "You're right. I need to stay positive. We'll be out in the open air before we know it, and everything is going to be great. Don't forget that the application and fee are due in a week, okay? Bye!"

6 Every July, Evergreen High School hosts a two-week camping trip for students. The trip is an opportunity to learn about the outdoors and build a community before the school year starts. Nora has made her most cherished memories in the great outdoors. She especially loves camp because it reminds her of when she used to go to state parks with her grandpa to bird-watch. It's because of him that she loves nature. Since he passed away five years ago, Nora has made it a point to get outside as much as possible. She even takes his old binoculars with her to camp so that she can observe the birds and other wildlife.

NOTES

7 Nora gives up searching for her socks and lies on the floor. Her mom shouts for her to come downstairs to talk. *What is it this time?* she thinks. *Did I forget to take out the trash? Was I supposed to clean the bathroom?* She closes her eyes, takes a deep breath, and imagines she is back at camp lying in the grass by the lake. She feels the mellow breeze glide across her bare arms and face. The pine trees dance in the wind as tiny rays of sunlight peek out through their branches. A blue jay swoops through the sky and lands in its nest. Nora wishes she could be free from worries, like the wildlife in the forest. She wants to rid herself of stress from family, school, and money. For now, summer camp is the closest she can get to independence. She opens her eyes. They take a moment to adjust to the artificial glare of her ceiling light. *I must get out of this house,* she thinks.

8 When Nora finally makes her way downstairs, she finds her mom sitting in the living room. She looks more tired than usual and wears a gloomy expression. "Why the sad face, Mom?" Nora jests.

9 "Honey, sit down. We need to talk." Nora sits on the couch across from her. "You are old enough now, so I'm going to jump straight to the point. I was laid off from my job at the nursing home this morning. Until I find a new job, I need you to pitch in and help with the bills." Her mother exhales and looks down at the floor. Nora is shocked. However, she isn't frightened the way she knows some of her friends would be. Nora and her mom have fallen on hard times in the past, but they have always come out on top.

10 "I'm sorry, Mom. I will help in any way I can," Nora says sincerely.

11 "Really? Thank you." Her mom's mood lightens.

12 "Of course. We need to stick together!" Nora exclaims. "I was going to get a summer job to keep me busy until camp anyway. Speaking of camp, I need to turn in my signed application and $250 fee soon. Do you have it ready?"

13 "Well, Nora, that's the problem. Money is tight now, so we can't afford to pay the fee."

14 Nora wants to yell and protest, but she knows that won't help the situation. *But you promised I could go,* she thinks. Instead, she says,

NOTES

"I understand. We'll figure something out." Nora smiles faintly, but tears begin to well in her eyes. She excuses herself from the room.

15 Back in her bedroom, Nora's thoughts race. *I can't believe this is happening. I deserve to go to camp just as much as my friends do. So much for one summer of freedom before adult responsibilities kick in. This summer is going to be the worst!*

16 Nora picks up her duffle bag and dumps its contents onto the floor. Amid the pile of sweatpants and t-shirts, she spots her grandpa's antique binoculars. *This isn't fair. Grandpa would want me to go to camp,* she thinks. Suddenly, she knows exactly what she has to do.

17 Nora puts the binoculars in her backpack, throws on her tennis shoes, and races downtown on her bike. She parks outside the local pawn shop. Then, clutching her backpack, she takes a deep breath and enters the shop. Nora glances around the room and notices the plethora of jewelry, electronics, and musical instruments. She imagines the histories of the abandoned items and their forgotten owners. *Will the memory of Grandpa and his love for nature be lost as well?*

18 A man emerges from the back of the store and asks if he can help her. Nora places her backpack on the counter and carefully removes the binoculars. She sees her reflection in the lens and realizes that selling the binoculars is wrong. Her grandfather's memory is worth much more than a quick payout and a summer away from home. Plus, if she went away, she'd abandon her mother, who needs her help.

19 "Uh, never mind," Nora stammers as she puts the binoculars away. On her way out the door, she sees a bulletin board covered with posts for job openings. A poster catches her eye. The local community center is looking for someone to lead nature walks and weekly birding outings. She takes the flyer and stuffs it in her backpack. As she bikes home, Nora cannot believe what she almost did. She realizes that a summer job is a much better solution to her problems. She might not be able to go to camp, but she will be free to be outside and share her love for the great outdoors.

WRITE

Writers often take notes about story ideas before they sit down to write. Think about what you've learned so far about organizing narrative writing to help you begin prewriting.

- **Audience:** Who is your audience, and what message do you want to express to your audience?
- **Purpose:** What kind of independence do you want to write about, and why is it desired?
- **Characters:** What types of characters would you like to write about in your narrative?
- **Setting:** Where and when will your story be set? How might the setting of your story affect the characters and problem?
- **Plot:** What challenges might these characters face? What events will lead to the resolution of the conflict while keeping a reader engaged?
- **Point of View:** From which point of view should your story be told, and why?
- **Theme/Reflection:** If you are writing an imagined narrative, what general message about life do you want to express? If you are writing a real narrative, what careful thoughts about the significance of your experience will you include?

Response Instructions

Use the questions in the bulleted list to write a one-paragraph summary. Your summary should describe what will happen in your narrative.

Don't worry about including all of the details now; focus only on the most essential and important elements. You will refer to this short summary as you continue through the steps of the writing process.

Skill: Organizing Narrative Writing

••• CHECKLIST FOR ORGANIZING NARRATIVE WRITING

As you consider how to organize your writing for your narrative, use the following questions as a guide:

- Who is the narrator, and who are the characters in the story?
- Where will the story take place?
- Have I created a problem that characters will have to face and resolve, while noting its significance to the characters?
- Have I created a smooth progression of experiences or plot events?

Here are some strategies to help you create a smooth progression of experiences or events in your narrative:

- Establish a context
  - > choose a setting and a problem that characters will have to face and resolve, noting its significance to the characters
  - > decide how the conflict will be resolved
    - o the problem often builds to a climax, when the characters are forced to take action
- Introduce a narrator and/or characters
  - > characters can be introduced all at once or over the course of the narrative
  - > choose the role each character will play in the story

YOUR TURN

Place each event, listed under Event Options, in the correct position in the narrative sequence by writing the corresponding letter in the chart below.

Event Options	
A	Sophie is going on a trip to California to visit her aunt. She is supposed to fly from Washington, D.C., to San Diego. Sophie is fifteen years old, and she has never traveled by plane. She is nervous about navigating the airport and flying alone.
B	There is little time left before her plane's departure. Sophie starts to think that her mom, dad, and aunt were wrong to believe she could do this alone. Then she sees an airport employee. She takes a deep breath.
C	Sophie's parents explain the process of checking in, getting through security, and finding the gate. They drop her off and hug her goodbye. Sophie is nervous but knows that her parents can't go with her beyond the security checkpoint anyway, so she has to do this herself.
D	Sophie passes through security and is immediately intimidated by the hordes of people in the terminal. Everyone seems to know exactly what to do and where to go. She asks a stranger for directions and ends up going the wrong way. Sophie gets lost in the airport with little time to board her flight. She is certain she is going to miss her flight to San Diego. She panics and frantically searches for a map.
E	Sophie relaxes. She asks the airport employee how to find her flight's gate. The employee gives her directions, and she makes it to the gate just in time. She realizes she has the ability to fly on her own after all.

Narrative Sequence	Event
Exposition	
Rising Action	
Climax	
Falling Action	
Resolution	

YOUR TURN

Complete the chart below by writing a short summary of what will happen in each section of your narrative.

Narrative Sequence	Event
Exposition	
Rising Action	
Climax	
Falling Action	
Resolution	

Narrative Writing Process: Draft

PLAN | DRAFT | REVISE | EDIT AND PUBLISH

You have already made progress toward writing your personal or fictional narrative. Now it is time to draft your personal or fictional narrative.

WRITE

Use your plan and other responses in your Binder to draft your narrative. You may also have new ideas as you begin drafting. Feel free to explore those new ideas as you have them. You can also ask yourself these questions to ensure that your writing is focused, organized, and detailed:

Draft Checklist:

- ☐ **Purpose and Focus:** Have I made the conflict clear to readers? Have I included only relevant information and details and nothing extraneous that might confuse my readers?
- ☐ **Organization:** Does the sequence of events in my story make sense? Will readers be engaged by the organization and want to keep reading to find out what happens next?
- ☐ **Ideas and Details:** Does my writing include engaging ideas and details? Will my readers be able to easily follow and understand descriptions of characters, settings, or events?

Before you submit your draft, read it over carefully. You want to be sure that you've responded to all aspects of the prompt.

Here is Daniel's narrative draft. As you read, notice how Daniel develops his draft to be focused, organized, and detailed. As he continues to revise and edit his narrative, he will find and improve weak spots in his writing, as well as correct any language or punctuation mistakes.

NOTES

STUDENT MODEL: FIRST DRAFT

The Price of Freedom

~~Nora is on the phone with her best friend, Simone.~~ Nora firmly presses her phone between her ear and shoulder. "I can't beleive this is our last summer at camp," she says as she digs through her dirty laundry hamper. "Simone, I have to put you on speaker phone." She sets her phone on the carpet. "Did you borrow my wool socks? I can't find them anywhere."

"Nope," she replies. Nora sighs. Wool socks are a must have for cold nights camping in the mountains. Camp doesn't start until a month from now, but already packing.

~~"We must make the most out of camp this year. This is our last summer. Then comes college, marriage, kids..."~~

~~"Please don't get serious again. This summer will be the best yet."~~

"We must make the most out of camp this year. This is our last summer before our senior year! Then comes college, marriage, kids . . . ," Simone hesitates. "Who knows if we'll ever be free of responsibility again?"

"No!" Nora cries. "Please don't get serious again. We are still kids! This summer will be the best yet."

"You're right. I need to stay positive. We'll be out in the open air before we know it, and everything is going to be great. Don't forget that the application and fee are due in a week, okay? Bye!"

Every july, Evergreen high school hosts a two-week camping trip for students. The trip is an opportunity to learn about the outdoors. The trip is also an opportunity to build a community before the school year starts. Nora has made her most cherished memories in the great outdoors. She especially loves camp because it reminds her of

Skill:
Story Beginnings

After reviewing the checklist for story beginnings, Daniel decides he could use techniques that are more creative to interest readers in his story. He starts the story in a more engaging way and uses dialogue to help set up the conflict.

NOTES

when she used to go to state parks with her Grandpa to bird-watch. It's because of him that she loved nature. Since he passed away five years ago, Nora had made it a point to get outside at much as possible. She even takes his old binoculars with her to camp so that she can observe the Birds and other Wildlife.

~~Nora gives up searching for her socks and lies on the floor. Her mom shouts for her to come downstairs to talk. *What is it this time?* she thinks. *Did I forget to take out the trash? Was I supposed to clean the bathroom?* She closes her eyes, takes a deep breath, and imagines she is back at camp lying in the grass by the lake. She feels the breeze on her arms and face. The pine trees sway in the wind and the sun shines. A blue jay flies through the sky and lands in its nest. Nora wishes she could be free from worries like the wildlife in the forest. She wants to rid herself of stress from family, school, and money. For now, summer camp is the closest she can get to independence. She opens her eyes. They take a moment to adjust to her ceiling light. *I must get out of this house*, she thinks.~~

Nora gives up searching for her socks and lies on the floor. Her mom shouts for her to come downstairs to talk. *What is it this time?* she thinks. *Did I forget to take out the trash? Was I supposed to clean the bathroom?* She closes her eyes, takes a deep breath, and imagines she is back at camp lying in the grass by the lake. She feels the mellow breeze glide across her bare arms and face. The pine trees dance in the wind as tiny rays of sunlight peek out through their branches. A blue jay swoops through the sky and lands in its nest. Nora wishes she could be free from worries, like the wildlife in the forest. She wants to rid herself of stress from family, school, and money. For now, summer camp is the closest she can get to independence. She opens her eyes. They take a moment to adjust to the artificial glare of her ceiling light. *I must get out of this house,* she thinks.

Skill: Descriptive Details

Daniel adds more descriptive language to enhance the sensory appeal of Nora's imagined scene. Touch details, such as "the mellow breeze," contribute to the mood of the scene. They help readers understand that Nora feels relaxed and free at camp.

When Nora finally makes her way downstairs, her mom sitting in the liveing room. She looks more tired than usual and wore a gloomy expression. "Why the sad face, Mom?" nora jests.

~~"Honey, sit down. We need to talk." Nora sits on the couch across from her. "You are old enough now, so I'm going to jump straight to the point. I was laid off from my job at the nurseing home this morning. Until I find~~

NOTES

~~a new job, I need you to pitch in and help with the bills." Her mother exhales and looks down at the floor. Nora is shocked. In addition, she isn't frightened the way she knows some of her friends would be.~~

"Honey, sit down. We need to talk." Nora sits on the couch across from her. "You are old enough now, so I'm going to jump straight to the point. I was laid off from my job at the nursing home this morning. Until I find a new job, I need you to pitch in and help with the bills." Her mother exhales and looks down at the floor. Nora is shocked. However, she isn't frightened the way she knows some of her friends would be. Nora and her mom have fallen on hard times in the past, but they have always come out on top.

Skill: Transitions

Daniel realizes he hasn't used the correct transition to show the relationship between ideas in two sentences. He has used in addition, *as if he were just adding information. He replaces that transition with* however *to set the ideas in opposition and stress that Nora's surprise is not accompanied by fear.*

"I'm sorry, Mom. I will help in any way I can," Nora says sincerely.

"Really? Thank you." Her mom's mood lightens.

"Of course. We need to stick together!" Nora exclaims. "I was going to get a summer job to keep me busy until camp anyway and speaking of camp I need to turn in my signed application and $250 fee soon. Do you have it ready?"

"Well, Nora, that's the problem. Money is tight now, so we can't afford to pay the fee."

~~Nora wants to yell and protest, but she knows that won't help the situation. She wants to remind her mom that she promised to sign the application and pay the fee. Instead, she says, "I understand. We'll figure something out." Nora smiles faintly, but tears begin to well in her eyes.~~

~~Nora's thoughts race. She can't believe this is happening to her. She deserves to go to camp just as much as her friends do. Nora was looking forward to one summer of freedom before adult responsibilities kick in. She decides that without camp, this summer is going to be the worst.~~

Nora wants to yell and protest, but she knows that won't help the situation. *But you promised I could go,* she thinks. Instead, she says, "I understand. We'll figure something out." Nora smiles faintly, but tears begin to well in her eyes. She excuses herself from the room.

Skill: Narrative Techniques

Daniel replaces his explanation of Nora's thoughts, after she learns that her mom can't afford to pay the camp fee, with her actual thoughts. He uses italics to show that these thoughts are a break from the conventional narration.

Back in her bedroom, Nora's thoughts race. *I can't believe this is happening. I deserve to go to camp just as much as my friends do. So much for one summer of freedom before adult responsibilities kick in. This summer is going to be the worst!*

Nora picks up her duffle bag and dumps its contents onto the floor. Amid the pile of sweatpants and t-shirts, she spots her Grandpa's antique binoculars. Suddenly, she knows exactly what she has to do.

Nora puts the binoculars in her the backpack. She parks outside the local pawn shop. Then, clutching her backpack, she takes a deep breath and enters the shop. Nora glances around the room and notices a bunch of jewelry, electronics, and musical instruments. *Will the memory of Grandpa and his love for nature be lost as well?*

A man emerges from the back of the store and asks if he can help her. Nora places her backpack on the counter and carefuly removes the binoculars. Her grandfather's memory is worth much more than a quick payout and a summer away from home. Plus, if she went away, she'd leave her mother who needs her help. She sees her reflection in the lens and realizes that selling the binoculars is wrong.

~~"Uh, never mind," Nora says as she puts the binoculars away. A poster catches her eye. On her way out the door, she sees a bulletin board covered with posts for job openings. The local community center is looking for someone to lead nature walks and weekly birding outings. She takes the flyer and stuffs it in her backpack. As she bikes home, Nora cannot believe what she almost did. She will realize that a summer job is a much better solution to her problems.~~

"Uh, never mind," Nora stammers as she puts the binoculars away. On her way out the door, she sees a bulletin board covered with posts for job openings. A poster catches her eye. The local community center is looking for someone to lead nature walks and weekly birding outings. She takes the flyer and stuffs it in her backpack. As she bikes home, Nora cannot believe what she almost did. She realizes that a summer job is a much better solution to her problems. She might not be able to go to camp, but she will be free to be outside and share her love for the great outdoors.

NOTES

Skill: Conclusions

Daniel thinks about how to summarize his narrative's message in his conclusion. He adds a final sentence to provide a sense of closure and conclusion for readers.

Skill: Story Beginnings

••• CHECKLIST FOR STORY BEGINNINGS

Before you write the beginning of your narrative, ask yourself the following questions:

- What information does my reader need to know at the beginning of the story about the narrator, main character, setting, and the character's conflict?
- What will happen to my character in the story?

There are many ways to help you engage and orient your reader. Here are some questions to help you set out a problem, situation, or observation as well as its significance and introduce a narrator and/or characters:

- Action
  > What action could help reveal information about my character or conflict?
  > How might an exciting moment or observation and its significance grab my reader's attention?
  > How could a character's reaction help set the mood?
- Description
  > Does my story take place in a special location or specific time period?
  > How can describing a location or character grab my reader's attention? What powerful emotions can I use?
- Dialogue
  > What dialogue would help my reader understand the setting or the conflict?
  > How could a character's internal thoughts provide information for my reader?
- Information
  > Would a surprising statement grab the reader's attention?
  > What details will help my reader understand the character, conflict, or setting?

YOUR TURN

Below is the revised beginning of Daniel's narrative. Choose the best answer to each question about his story beginning.

> Nora firmly presses her phone between her ear and shoulder. "I can't believe this is our last summer at camp," she says as she digs through her dirty laundry hamper. "Simone, I have to put you on speaker phone." She sets her phone on the carpet. "Did you borrow my wool socks? I can't find them anywhere."
>
> "Nope," Simone replies. Nora sighs. Wool socks are a must have for cold nights camping in the mountains. Camp doesn't start until a month from now, but she's already packing.

1. Which line could you add to the first paragraph to better show the contrast between the initial setting and camp?

   - ○ A. Nora's ear aches as she struggles to hear Simone through the worn-out phone receiver.
   - ○ B. Nora perks up when she realizes that maybe the socks are in the basement.
   - ○ C. Nora smiles as she thinks of the fresh air of camp and holds her breath, digging deeper into the hamper.
   - ○ D. Nora is distracted from her search for wool socks as her stomach growls for a snack.

2. In the second paragraph, how does the detail "Camp doesn't start until a month from now, but she's already packing" help the reader better understand the main character?

   - ○ A. It illustrates Nora's level of excitement about camp.
   - ○ B. It shows that Nora is a very disorganized person and packing will take her a long time.
   - ○ C. It characterizes Nora as anxious.
   - ○ D. It shows that Nora does not want to go to camp.

WRITE

Use the questions in the checklist to revise the beginning of your narrative.

Skill: Narrative Techniques

••• CHECKLIST FOR NARRATIVE TECHNIQUES

As you begin to develop the techniques you will use in your narrative, ask yourself the following questions:

- Is it clear which character is talking in a dialogue?
- Is the pacing of events suitable and effective?
- Which literary devices can strengthen descriptions of the characters or plot events? How can I use personal reflection to develop my narrative?
- What additional characters and/or events might help to develop the narrative?

Here are some methods that can help you use dialogue, description, pacing, reflection, and multiple plot lines to develop experiences, events, and/or characters in your narrative:

- use character dialogue to explain events or actions
  - > use quotation marks correctly
  - > include identifying names as needed before or after quotation marks
- use description so the reader can visualize the characters, setting, and other elements
  - > descriptions should contribute to the reader's understanding of the element being described
- use pacing effectively
  - > for a quick pace, use limited description, short paragraphs, brief dialogue, and simpler sentences
  - > for a slower pace, use detailed description, longer paragraphs, and complex sentence structures
- use reflection to comment on the overall message
  - > include a character's personal inner thoughts or insights
- create multiple plot lines that further develop the narrative's message
  - > include characters, events, or other elements that will further develop the plot
- use any combination of the techniques above

YOUR TURN

Choose the best answer to each question.

1. Below is a section from a previous draft of Daniel's story, in which he wants to include Nora's thoughts to enhance the narration. How should he rewrite the underlined sentence to accurately show Nora's thoughts in this moment?

> Nora catches the pawn shop owner eyeing her grandpa's binoculars. His face lights up. She wonders how much he is willing to pay for them. <u>Nora wishes she researched how much they are worth before hastily riding her bike downtown to the shop.</u> Nora hopes he doesn't try to sell her short.
>
> "How did you manage to get your hands on that pair of binoculars, Miss?" he says curiously.

- ○ A. If only Nora knew how much the binoculars were worth.
- ○ B. *I should have researched the value of the binoculars before coming here,* she thinks.
- ○ C. She thinks about how she should have researched how much the binoculars are worth.
- ○ D. *What if the binoculars aren't worth as much as I thought?*

2. Daniel wants to add details to a previous draft to develop the relationship between characters. Which sentence should he add between sentences 1 and 2 below to further describe how the characters relate to one another?

> (1) Nora and Simone have known each other since kindergarten, but they did not become friends until their first summer at camp. (2) Since then, they have been inseparable.

- ○ A. They shared a cabin with seven other girls and a counselor.
- ○ B. They took swimming lessons and practiced archery.
- ○ C. They were fourteen years old.
- ○ D. They instantly clicked because they share an appreciation for the great outdoors.

WRITE

Use the questions in the checklist for narrative techniques to revise a section of your fictional or personal narrative.

Skill: Transitions

••• CHECKLIST FOR TRANSITIONS

Before you revise your current draft to include transitions, think about:

- the order of plot events
- how events build to create a unified story, build a specific mood, and work toward a particular outcome

Next, reread your current draft and note areas in your narrative where:

- the order of events is unclear or illogical
- changes in time or setting are confusing or unclear. Look for:
  - sudden jumps
  - missing or illogical plot events or outcome(s)
  - moments where the mood does not connect to the development of plot events

Revise your draft to use a variety of techniques to sequence events so that they build on one another to create a coherent whole and build toward a particular mood and outcome, using the following questions as a guide:

- What other techniques could I use so that events in my story build on one another, creating a coherent whole?
- Does the sequence of events in my story build toward a particular mood and outcome?
  - For example, you can build the mood of your story by creating a sense of mystery or suspense.
  - For example, you can build toward a particular outcome by showing character growth or by developing a resolution.
- Are there better transitional words, phrases, or clauses that I can use to show shifts in time or setting and relationships between experiences and events?

YOUR TURN

Choose the best answer to each question about Daniel's final draft of his narrative (see the Plan lesson).

1. Which of the following sentences from Daniel's story best illustrates a transition that helps Daniel build toward a consistent theme throughout the narrative?

   - O A. "*I must get out of this house*, she thinks."
   - O B. "'I'm sorry, Mom. I will help in any way I can,' Nora says sincerely."
   - O C. "Camp doesn't start until a month from now, but she's already packing."
   - O D. "She might not be able to go to camp, but she will be free to be outside and share her love for the great outdoors."

2. What effect does the use of the transition word *then* have in this sentence from paragraph 17 of Daniel's story: "Then, clutching her backpack, she takes a deep breath and enters the shop."

   - O A. It lets the reader know that Nora is having second thoughts about the pawn shop.
   - O B. It shows how much Nora does not want to go into the pawn shop.
   - O C. It pivots the reader toward Nora's decision to go to the pawn shop, emphasizing a major event or moment in the plot.
   - O D. It reinforces the theme of Nora's making tough decisions.

WRITE

Use the questions in the checklist to revise the transitions in your narrative.

Skill: Descriptive Details

••• CHECKLIST FOR DESCRIPTIVE DETAILS

First, reread the draft of your narrative and identify the following:

- places where descriptive details are needed to convey experiences and events
- vague, general, or overused words and phrases
- places where you want to tell how something looks, sounds, feels, smells, or tastes, such as:
  > experiences
  > events
  > settings
  > characters

Use telling details, sensory language, and precise words and phrases to convey a vivid picture of the experiences, events, setting, and/or characters, using the following questions as a guide:

- What experiences and events do I want to convey in my writing?
- Have I included telling details that help reveal the experiences and events in the story?
- How do I want the characters and setting portrayed?
- How can I use sensory language—or words that appeal to the sense of sight, sound, touch, smell, or taste—so that readers can clearly visualize the experiences, events, setting, and/or characters in my story?
- What can I refine or revise in my word choice to make sure the reader can picture what is taking place?

YOUR TURN

Choose the best answer to each question.

1. Daniel would like to add a descriptive smell detail to this sentence from a previous draft. Which sentence best adds a smell detail to his sentence?

> Nora enters the pawn shop.

- ○ A. Nora tries to enter the pawn shop, but the door is locked.
- ○ B. Nora feels a sticky substance on the door handle as she enters the pawn shop.
- ○ C. As Nora enters the pawn shop, she is overwhelmed by the distinct aroma of mothballs.
- ○ D. Nora enters the pawn shop only to find her mom crying as she talks to the owner.

2. Daniel wants to add a sensory detail to this passage from a previous draft to better establish the mood of the scene. What sentence can he add to help communicate an uplifting mood?

> *This job is perfect for me!* she thinks. Nora hastily stuffs the job posting into her backpack and hops on her bike. She rides home to deliver the news to her mom.

- ○ A. The sun burns brightly, guiding Nora on her way.
- ○ B. Nora is startled by a car horn and nearly falls.
- ○ C. Nora splashes through a pothole full of dirty water.
- ○ D. Nora feels the heat from the sun radiate off the asphalt.

WRITE

Use the questions in the checklist for descriptive details to revise a section of your fictional or personal narrative.

Skill: Conclusions

••• CHECKLIST FOR CONCLUSIONS

Before you write your conclusion, ask yourself the following questions:

- What important details should I include in the summary in my conclusion?
- What other thoughts and feelings could the characters share with readers in the conclusion?
- Should I express the importance of the events in my narrative through dialogue or a character's actions?

Below are two strategies to help you provide a conclusion that follows from and reflects on what is experienced, observed, or resolved over the course of the narrative:

- Peer Discussion
  > After you have written your introduction and body paragraphs, talk with a partner about possible endings for your narrative.
  > Review your notes, and think about how you want to end your story.
  > Briefly summarize the events in the narrative through the narrator or one of the characters.
  > Describe the narrator's observations about events in the narrative.
  > Reveal to readers why the experiences in the narrative matter through a character's reflections or resolutions.
  > Write your conclusion.
- Freewriting
  > Freewrite for 10 minutes about what you might include in your conclusion.
  > Review your notes, and think about how you want to end your story.
  > Briefly summarize the events in the narrative through the narrator or one of the characters.
  > Describe the narrator's observations about events in the narrative.
  > Reveal to readers why the experiences in the narrative matter through a character's reflections or resolutions.
  > Write your conclusion.

YOUR TURN

Below is the revised conclusion of Daniel's narrative. Choose the best answer to each question about his concluding paragraphs.

> A man emerges from the back of the store and asks if he can help her. Nora places her backpack on the counter and carefully removes the binoculars. She sees her reflection in the lens and realizes that selling the binoculars is wrong. Her grandfather's memory is worth much more than a quick payout and a summer away from home. Plus, if she went away, she'd abandon her mother, who needs her help.
>
> "Uh, never mind," Nora stammers as she puts the binoculars away. On her way out the door, she sees a bulletin board covered with posts for job openings. A poster catches her eye. The local community center is looking for someone to lead nature walks and weekly birding outings. She takes the flyer and stuffs it in her backpack. As she bikes home, Nora cannot believe what she almost did. She realizes that a summer job is a much better solution to her problems. She might not be able to go to camp, but she will be free to be outside and share her love for the great outdoors.

1. What is the effect of mentioning Nora's grandfather in the conclusion of the story?

   - ○ A. It shows that Nora really misses her grandfather and thinks of him often.
   - ○ B. It conveys to the reader how desperate Nora is to get to camp.
   - ○ C. It illustrates the theme that family is more important than camp by showing why Nora makes an important decision.
   - ○ D. It reinforces the value Nora's family places on the outdoors.

2. Which sentence from the revised conclusion best shows what Nora learned?

   - ○ A. "She realizes that a summer job is a much better solution to her problems."
   - ○ B. "She might not be able to go to camp, but she will be free to be outside and share her love for the great outdoors."
   - ○ C. "She sees her reflection in the lens and realizes that selling the binoculars is wrong."
   - ○ D. "Plus, if she went away, she'd abandon her mother, who needs her help."

WRITE

Use the questions in the checklist for conclusions to revise the ending of your narrative.

Narrative Writing Process: Revise

PLAN | DRAFT | REVISE | EDIT AND PUBLISH

You have written a draft of your fictional or personal narrative. You have also received input from your peers about how to improve it. Now you are going to revise your draft.

REVISION GUIDE

Examine your draft to find areas for revision. Keep in mind your purpose and audience as you revise for clarity, development, organization, and style. Use the guide below to help you review:

Review	Revise	Example
	Clarity	
Label parts of the narration that signal the characters' locations or movement between locations.	Insert words or phrases to better establish the setting and the transition between settings.	Nora puts the binoculars in her backpack, throws on her tennis shoes, and races downtown on her bike. She parks outside the local pawn shop. Then, clutching her backpack, she takes a deep breath and enters the shop.
	Development	
Identify moments in which your characters respond to conflict. Annotate moments where a character's reaction is confusing or unclear.	Focus on a single event and add details that show the motivation behind the character's reaction.	Nora is shocked. ~~In addition,~~ However, she isn't frightened the way she knows some of her friends would be. Nora and her mom have fallen on hard times in the past, but they have always come out on top. "I'm sorry, Mom. I will help in any way I can," Nora says sincerely.

Review	Revise	Example
Organization		
Explain your story in one or two sentences. Reread and annotate any places that don't match your explanation.	Rewrite the events in the correct sequence. Delete events and details that are not essential to the story, including any redundant description.	~~Nora is on the phone with her best friend, Simone.~~ Nora firmly presses her phone between her ear and shoulder. "I can't believe this is our last summer at camp," she says as she digs through her dirty laundry hamper. "Simone, I have to put you on speaker phone."
Style: Word Choice		
Identify each piece of dialogue that uses the word *says*.	Select pieces of dialogue to rewrite using action verbs.	"Uh, never mind," Nora ~~says~~ stammers as she puts the binoculars away.
Style: Sentence Fluency		
Read aloud your writing and listen to the way the text sounds. Does it sound choppy? Or does it flow smoothly with rhythm, movement, and emphasis on important details and events?	Rewrite a key event, making your sentences longer or shorter to achieve a better flow of writing and the emotion you want your reader to feel.	"This is our last ~~summer.~~ summer before our senior year! Then comes college, marriage, kids. . . ," Simone hesitates. "Who knows if we'll ever be free of responsibility again?" "No!" Nora cries. "Please don't get serious again. We are still kids! This summer will be the best yet."

WRITE

Use the revision guide, as well as your peer reviews, to help you evaluate your fictional or personal narrative to determine areas that should be revised.

Grammar: Capitalization

Proper nouns should always be capitalized. If the noun is composed of several words, do not capitalize articles (*a, an, the*), coordinating conjunctions (*and, but, for, or, nor, yet*), or prepositions of fewer than five letters. Capitalize a title showing family relationship when used with or in place of a proper noun. Do not capitalize it when preceded by an article or a possessive noun or pronoun.

Susanna Walcott's here from **Doctor Griggs.** The Crucible	The grass-plot before the jail, in **Prison Lane**, on a certain summer morning, not less than two centuries ago, was occupied by a pretty large number of the inhabitants of **Boston**, ... The Scarlet Letter	Because her leg did not improve but swelled more and more, the doctors at the school bound it with crude splints and took her by car, on September 9th, to the **Red Cross Hospital** in Hiroshima. Hiroshima

Salutations and closings require capitalization as well. Capitalize the first word of the salutation and the recipient's first and last names. Additionally, capitalize the first word of the closing of a letter.

Dear **M**iss **B**reed, **G**reetings from far-off Poston, Arizona! Dear Miss Breed	**Y**ours very truly, Einstein's Letter to the President	**T**o the Editor of the New York Times: The Case of Susan B. Anthony

Direct quotations appear in quotation marks. If a quotation is a complete sentence, the first word of the quotation should be capitalized even if the quotation appears in the middle of a sentence, but do not capitalize the first word of a quotation that cannot stand as a complete sentence.

As Bacon said of manners, "To obtain them, it only needs not to despise them," so we say of animal spirits, that they are the spontaneous product of health and of a social habit. Society and Solitude	This common response to unfulfilled expectations is known as the "frustration-aggression hypothesis." Dumped!

YOUR TURN

1. How should this sentence be changed?

> My Sister told me that Richard joined the peace corps and would be going to Ghana.

- ○ A. Lowercase **sister.**
- ○ B. Capitalize **peace corps.**
- ○ C. Lowercase **Ghana.**
- ○ D. Answers A and B are correct.

2. How should this closing be changed?

> With Great Admiration,

- ○ A. Change the word **Great** to **great.**
- ○ B. Change the words **Great Admiration** to **great admiration.**
- ○ C. Change the word **With** to **with.**
- ○ D. No change needs to be made to this closing.

3. How should this sentence be changed?

> Muir remembers his journey to America in 1849 with his brothers and father as "The first grand adventure of my life."

- ○ A. Capitalize **journey.**
- ○ B. Capitalize **brothers** and **father.**
- ○ C. Do not capitalize **The.**
- ○ D. No change needs to be made to this sentence.

4. How should this sentence be changed?

> *Metamorphoses,* the Roman poet Ovid's fascinating retelling of the daphne and Phoebus myth, is based on earlier Greek tales.

- ○ A. Make **Roman** lowercase.
- ○ B. Capitalize **fascinating.**
- ○ C. Capitalize **daphne.**
- ○ D. No change needs to be made to this sentence.

Grammar: Consistent Verb Tenses

The tense of a verb should remain consistently in the past, present, or future, as the action is placed.

When writing about two or more events that occur at the same time, do not shift, or change, tenses. If verb tense is inconsistent, it is difficult for the reader to know when something happened.

Correct	Incorrect
We planned a picnic, but the rain forced us to postpone it.	We planned a picnic, but the rain forces us to postpone it.

It is possible to have more than one tense in a sentence, but it must be clear why there is a difference.

Rule	Text
It is possible to have different tenses in a sentence if the shift in tenses shows that one event precedes or follows another in time.	She did not hear the story as many women have heard the same, with a paralyzed inability to accept its significance. The Story of an Hour
A present-tense verb can express a general truth even if the rest of the sentence is not in the present.	We hold these truths to be self-evident, that all men are created equal, that they are endowed by their Creator with certain unalienable Rights, that among these are Life, Liberty, and the pursuit of Happiness. The Declaration of Independence
Even when there are several verbs in a long sentence, the verb tenses need to remain consistent if they are showing action over a consistent period of time.	When Lee came to the sentence about the officers' side-arms, private horses, and baggage, he showed for the first time during the reading of the letter a slight change of countenance, and was evidently touched by this act of generosity. Lee Surrenders to Grant, April 9th, 1865

YOUR TURN

1. Decide whether the verb tenses are consistent. If not, pick the change that will make the sentence correct.

   Lou Gehrig was a legendary baseball player in the 1930s; he hits four home runs in one game.

   - ○ A. Change **was** to **is**.
   - ○ B. Change **hits** to **hit**.
   - ○ C. Change **hits** to **will hit**.
   - ○ D. No change needs to be made to this sentence.

2. Decide whether the verb tenses are consistent. If not, pick the change that will make the sentence correct.

   Sadly, a terrible neurological disease would cut his career short, and his name would become associated with the disease: Lou Gehrig's disease.

   - ○ A. Change **would cut** to **cuts**.
   - ○ B. Change **would become** to **becomes**.
   - ○ C. Change **would become** to **will become**.
   - ○ D. No change needs to be made to this sentence.

3. Decide whether the verb tenses are consistent. If not, pick the change that will make the sentence correct.

   Gehrig gives a famous speech on July 4, 1939, and said good-bye to all his fans and called himself the luckiest man in the world.

   - ○ A. Change **gives** to **gave**.
   - ○ B. Change **said** to **says**.
   - ○ C. Change **called** to **will call**.
   - ○ D. No change needs to be made to this sentence.

Grammar: Basic Spelling Rules

Rule	Text
When adding a suffix that begins with a vowel to a word that ends with a silent **e**, usually drop the **e**.	Lee now looked greatly relieved, and though anything but a **demonstrative** man, he gave every evidence of his **appreciation** of this concession, and said, "This will have the best possible effect upon the men. It will be very gratifying and will do much toward **conciliating** our people." Lee Surrenders to Grant, April 9th, 1865
When a word ends in a consonant + *y*, change the *y* to *i* before adding a suffix.	America is rapidly losing its position as leader of the world simply because the Democratic Administration has **pitifully** failed to provide effective leadership. Remarks to the Senate in Support of a Declaration of Conscience
When adding ***-ly*** to a word that ends in a single ***l,*** keep the ***l***.	I looked around and up at Mr. Cunningham, whose face was **equally** impassive. To Kill a Mockingbird
Generally, double the final consonant if the last syllable of the word is accented or if the word ends in a single consonant preceded by a single vowel and the accent does not move after the suffix is added.	The effect of this separation on their educational opportunities was well stated by a finding in the Kansas case by a court which nevertheless felt **compelled** to rule against the Negro plaintiffs. Brown v. Board of Education

YOUR TURN

1. How should this sentence be changed?

   Despite David's efforts at being careful, he dropped his eyeglasses and the lenses shatterred.

   - A. Change **dropped** to **droped.**
   - B. Change **eyeglasses** to **eye glasses.**
   - C. Change **shatterred** to **shattered.**
   - D. No change needs to be made to this sentence.

2. How should this sentence be changed?

   The largest assemblely of competitors gathered in Munich, Germany, which showcased ten thousand athletes in 1972.

   - A. Change **gathered** to **gatherred.**
   - B. Change **assemblely** to **assembly.**
   - C. Change **showcased** to **showcaseed.**
   - D. No change needs to be made to this sentence.

3. How should the spelling errors in this sentence be corrected?

   The valueable lessons to be learned from studying any historical event are made more meaningful by comparing and contrasting varyous historyans' interpretations of the same event.

   - A. Change **valueable** to **valuable.**
   - B. Change **historyans'** to **historians'.**
   - C. Change **varyous** to **various.**
   - D. Choices A, B, and C are all correct.

4. How should the spelling error in this sentence be corrected?

   The representative of the crown was busy decreing this and that and did not notice the fulminating fury of the burgeoning crowd beneath the balcony.

   - A. Change **representative** to **representetive.**
   - B. Change **decreing** to **decreeing.**
   - C. Change **fulminating** to **fulminateing.**
   - D. No change needs to be made to this sentence.

Narrative Writing Process: Edit and Publish

PLAN | DRAFT | REVISE | EDIT AND PUBLISH

You have revised your fictional or personal narrative based on your peer feedback and your own examination.

Now, it is time to edit your narrative. When you revised, you focused on the content of your narrative. You probably looked at your story's beginning, descriptive details, and conclusion. When you edit, you focus on the mechanics of your story, paying close attention to things like grammar and punctuation.

Use the checklist below to guide you as you edit:

- ☐ Have I correctly capitalized words?
- ☐ Have I used a consistent verb tense throughout the story?
- ☐ Do I have any sentence fragments or run-on sentences?
- ☐ Have I spelled everything correctly?

Notice some edits Daniel has made:

- Added a subject and verb to correct a sentence fragment
- Corrected the spelling of a word ending in silent *e* when adding a suffix that begins with a vowel
- Changed a verb's tense to maintain consistency
- Capitalized a proper noun

> When Nora finally makes her way downstairs, she finds her mom sitting in the ~~liveing~~ living room. She looks more tired than usual and ~~wore~~ wears a gloomy expression. "Why the sad face, Mom?" ~~nora~~ Nora jests.

WRITE

Use the questions on the previous page, as well as your peer reviews, to help you evaluate your personal or fictional narrative to determine areas that need editing. Then, edit your narrative to correct those errors.

Once you have made all your corrections, you are ready to publish your work. You can distribute your writing to family and friends, hang it on a bulletin board, or post it on your blog. If you publish online, share the link with your family, friends, and classmates.

PHOTO/IMAGE CREDITS:

cover, iStock.com/DNY59
p. iii, iStock.com/DNY59
p. ix, iStock.com/DNY59
p. x, Abigail Adams - Universal History Archive/Getty
p. x, Anne Bradstreet - Public Domain
p. x, Maryse Condé - Eric Fougere/Contributor/Getty
p. x, Olaudah Equiano - Fotosearch/Stringer/Getty
p. x, Benjamin Franklin - Public Domain
p. xi, Nathaniel Hawthorne - MPI/Stringer/Archive Photos Collection/Getty
p. xi, Thomas Jefferson - Stock Montage/Contributor/Archive Photos/Getty
p. xi, David McCullough - Boston Globe/Contributor/Getty
p. xi, Arthur Miller - Bettmann/Contributor/Bettmann/Getty
p. xi, Phillis Wheatley - Hulton Archive/Culture Club/Contributor/Getty Images
p. xii, istock.com/drnadig
p. 1, Culture Club/Hulton Archive/Getty Images
p. 4, DEA PICTURE LIBRARY/De Agostini/Getty Images
p. 5, Education Images/Universal Images Group/Getty Images
p. 7, istock.com/drnadig
p. 8, iStock.com/ihoe
p. 13, iStock.com/ihoe
p. 14, iStock.com/ThomasVogel
p. 15, iStock.com/ThomasVogel
p. 16, iStock.com/ihoe
p. 17, iStock.com/KenWiedemann
p. 22, iStock.com/
p. 23, G. Greene/Conde Nast Collection/Getty Images
p. 25, iStock.com/razumaria
p. 26, Public Domain Image
p. 29, iStock.com/dan_prat
p. 33, iStock.com/Sjo
p. 41, iStock.com/Sjo
p. 42, iStock/Spanishalex
p. 43, iStock/Spanishalex
p. 44, iStock.com/urbancow
p. 45, iStock.com/urbancow
p. 46, iStock.com/Sjo
p. 47, Geography Photos/Universal Images Group Editorial/GettyImages
p. 48, Encyclopedia Britannica/Universal Images Group/Getty Images
p. 51, Geography Photos/Universal Images Group Editorial/GettyImages
p. 52, iStock.com/Paul Calbar
p. 53, iStock/mashuk
p. 54, iStock/kutaytanir
p. 58, iStock/kutaytanir
p. 59, iStock.com/Martin Barraud
p. 60, iStock.com/Martin Barraud
p. 61, iStock/kutaytanir
p. 62, Christine Glade/iStock.com
p. 66, iStock.com/rustyl3599
p. 71, ©iStock.com/Royce DeGrie
p. 72, iStock/THEPALMER
p. 76, ©iStock.com/Royce DeGrie
p. 77, iStock.com/Brostock
p. 78, iStock.com/Brostock
p. 79, iStock.com/pixhook
p. 80, iStock.com/pixhook
p. 81, iStock.com/ThomasVogel
p. 82, iStock.com/ThomasVogel
p. 83, ©iStock.com/Royce DeGrie
p. 84, iStock.com/
p. 87, iStock.com/
p. 88, iStock.com/eskaylim
p. 89, iStock.com/eskaylim
p. 90, iStock.com/
p. 91, catunchik/alekseystemmer
p. 97, iStock.com/hanibaram, iStock.com/seb_ra, iStock.com/Martin Barraud
p. 98, iStock.com/Martin Barraud
p. 104, iStock.com/oonal
p. 107, iStock.com/Martin Barraud
p. 112, iStock.com/truelight
p. 114, iStock.com/Jinnawat
p. 116, iStock.com/Jeff_Hu
p. 118, iStock/Jasmina007
p. 120, iStock.com/stevedangers
p. 122, iStock.com/Martin Barraud
p. 124, iStock.com/thinkreaction
p. 126, iStock.com/peeterv
p. 128, iStock.com/efks
p. 130, iStock.com/Martin Barraud

Text Fulfillment Through StudySync

studysync

If you are interested in specific titles, please fill out the form below and we will check availability through our partners.

ORDER DETAILS

Date:

TITLE	AUTHOR	Paperback/ Hardcover	Specific Edition *If Applicable*	Quantity

SHIPPING INFORMATION

Contact:

Title:

School/District:

Address Line 1:

Address Line 2:

Zip or Postal Code:

Phone:

Mobile:

Email:

BILLING INFORMATION

☐ *SAME AS SHIPPING*

Contact:

Title:

School/District:

Address Line 1:

Address Line 2:

Zip or Postal Code:

Phone:

Mobile:

Email:

PAYMENT INFORMATION

☐ CREDIT CARD

Name on Card:

Card Number: Expiration Date: Security Code:

☐ PO

Purchase Order Number:

StudySync Text Fulfillment, BookheadEd Learning, LLC
610 Daniel Young Drive | Sonoma, CA 95476